LEAN FOR LIFE

Other books by Clarence Bass

RIPPED

The Sensible Way to Achieve Ultimate Muscularity

RIPPED2

The all-new companion volume to RIPPED

RIPPED3

The Recipes, The Routines and The Reasons

THE LEAN ADVANTAGE

Four years of the Ripped Question and Answer Department

THE LEAN ADVANTAGE2

The Second Four Years

THE LEAN ADVANTAGE3

Four More Years

Challenge Yourself
Leanness, Fitness & Health at any age

The author in top bodybuilding shape. *Photo by Allen Hughes.*

LEAN FOR LIFE

By Clarence Bass

Stay
motivated
and lean
forever

Clarence Bass' **RIPPED**™ Enterprises
Albuquerque, New Mexico

ISBN–13: 978–0–9609714–5–9
ISBN–10: 0–9609714–5–9

Fourth Printing 2007

Published by Clarence Bass' Ripped Enterprises
P.O. Box 51236
Albuquerque, New Mexico 87181-1236 USA
(505) 266-5858   FAX 1-505-266-9123

RIPPED™ is the trademark of Clarence and Carol Bass

Library of Congress Catalog card number: 91–90779

ISBN–13: 978–0–9609714–5–9
ISBN–10: 0–9609714–5–9

Composition by Wright Graphics
Albuquerque, New Mexico

Manufactured by Thomson-Shore, Inc.
Dexter, Michigan

Photos on front and back cover by Chris Lund

I dedicate this book to Guy Trucano Jr. For years, Guy typed (and retyped) my books, columns and correspondence. His goal was to finish this book before succumbing to cancer... and he almost made it. Our communication was practically all second-hand, me on the dictating machine and Guy on the keyboard, but still we became great friends. My dictation almost invariably came back with a long note from Guy. He had a unique perspective on the world and an opinion on just about everything, plus he had a rare — often humorous — way of expressing himself. Yes, he definitely had a way with words. Guy was a lovable old curmudgeon. I miss him.

ACKNOWLEDGMENTS

Harriet Moldov and Carole Wright again prepared my manuscript for the printer. We have now worked together on five books, and I learn to appreciate their skills more each time. Harriet is known as "Golden Fingers," and I was reminded why as I proofread the galleys. Her accuracy is truly amazing. Carole, who now does business as Wright Graphics, worked from dawn to dusk for days on end to prepare the manuscript in camera-ready form. I believe this is her best effort. Harriet and Carole, I thank you one more time.

David Prokop, like Carole and Harriet (and Guy Trucano Jr.), has worked on most of my other books, but the broader scope of this book made his contribution more valuable than before. On my earlier books, Dave edited the manuscript after it was completed. On this book, Dave was involved from the start. I sent each chapter to him as it was written, and his comments and suggestions have, I believe, made this book more useful to the general public, even sedentary beginners. If this book successfully treads the line in satisfying a broader audience, Dave's input is one of the reasons. (If it fails, of course, the responsibility is mine alone.) What's more, Dave's editing pencil once again made my manuscript easier to read and understand.

Finally, I thank my wife Carol. She is both my number-one supporter and my severest critic. Even though her plate was already full, when Guy Trucano passed away, she stepped in and typed the final chapters of this book through many revisions. She did much more than that, however. She was my sounding board, telling me when something did not ring true. In my case, that's not easy, because I don't always take criticism well. She stood her ground, however, and told me what I needed to hear. I couldn't get along without you, Carol. I love you.

WARNING

Any application of the recommendations set forth in the following pages is at the reader's discretion and sole risk. The information in this book is intended for people in good health. Anyone with medical problems — of any nature — should see a doctor before starting a diet and exercise program. Furthermore, even if you have no known health problems, it is advisable to consult your doctor before making major changes in your lifestyle.

Invariably, if you are out of shape and want to start training, follow the advice of the American Medical Association: "Start *slowly* and increase the vigor and duration of the activity as your fitness improves."

CONTENTS

INTRODUCTION

There are only two things you really need to know to get into the proper frame of mind to read this book:

- Statistics show that 95% of the people who lose weight through dieting gain all the weight back (and usually more) soon after they go off the diet. In other words, diets don't work!
- About a decade ago Clarence Bass was able to reduce his body fat level to 2.4% *without really trying* — no calorie counting, no deprivation, no starvation, no dieting. And by following the lifestyle approach he describes in great detail in *Lean For Life*, he's kept his body fat level below 5-6% constantly since then!

Think of it! It's truly difficult to believe — in a country where thousands of people are overweight and struggle valiantly, and usually unsuccessfully, to lose weight permanently on various diets, where many athletes go through a self-imposed nutritional purgatory to pare their weight down to a fine competitive edge (sometimes even resorting to starvation or bulimia) — that Clarence Bass was able to reduce his body fat level down to 2.4% *without trying!*

(By the way, if you don't already know it, a 2.4% body fat level is ultra low — about as low as anybody would probably want or need to go. As an example, world-class male marathon runners usually average 6% body fat; elite women marathoners somewhat higher since women genetically carry more fat on their body.)

I've known Clarence Bass since 1980, when he first started writing his popular "Ripped" column that appears monthly in *Muscle & Fitness* magazine. Since that time Clarence, a lawyer by profession and a lifelong weight trainer and (now) health-and-fitness writer by avocation, has self-published five books on his all-round nutrition/exercise/health approach. *Lean For Life* is his sixth book and, in terms of its potential benefits to the general public, it's unquestionably his best and most valuable book yet!

I must confess that, for a long time, when I read about the low body fat level Clarence was able to maintain week in, week out, year after year, I thought he had to be a man of monumental discipline. How else could a person stay so super lean so consistently? I reasoned. Only through nerves of steel when it came to denying yourself food.

1

Only later did I come to discover that his secret is not willpower, nor calorie counting, nor starvation, nor fanatical exercise regimens (although, obviously, he does exercise). It's lifestyle. It's common sense and practicality applied ingeniously to nutrition and exercise. In fact, his approach is so effective, it all but takes willpower out of the picture. As I said, ingenious!

I once wrote of him: "I think Clarence Bass' real genius is that he's developed a way to thoroughly enjoy his diet and exercise program while staying consistently at 5% body fat or lower!"

Lean For Life is not a diet book; it is a lifestyle book. Which is good news if you have a weight problem or want to get ultra lean, because experts now agree that where permanent weight loss is concerned, lifestyle is the only approach that works. Clarence Bass is the acknowledged master at keeping his body lean and muscular. And anyone who follows his approach will achieve similar results, I'm convinced, because his common-sense, systematic, lifestyle (or nutrition and exercise) approach is all but guaranteed to work, whereas diets based on denial are almost guaranteed to fail.

How Clarence Bass got down to 2.4% body fat about a decade ago and has stayed relatively close to that level ever since — without starvation, without deprivation or denial, and without exotic amounts of exercise — is by following a healthy lifestyle, which in his case means "a three-pronged approach," to use his words, "a good diet, weight training and aerobics." With those elements neatly in place, the ultra-low body fat reading came as a natural but hidden benefit.

All three parts of his approach go together — like pieces of a jigsaw puzzle that just naturally fit. Here, in brief, is how and why his approach works:

• **Nutrition** — No one can stay on a diet for long if the diet is restrictive or severe. At the same time it's important to keep your calorie consumption down to a reasonable and appropriate level. The solution: eat a diet high in fiber and natural foods which are filling but don't contain many calories, or, as Clarence puts it: "My dietary approach is eating the right type of foods so you can eat a lot and never go away from the table feeling hungry or deprived, yet you keep your caloric consumption down."

• **Weight training** — Muscle burns more calories than fat at rest. So the more muscle you have relative to fat, the more calories your body burns in a resting state, and that can really add up over the course of a day. The best way to build and maintain muscle mass: weight training.

• **Aerobics** — Aerobic exercise not only burns a lot of calories when you're actually working out (many more calories than a basically high-intensity, anaerobic activity like weight training), but it also trains the body to burn fat more effectively. So aerobic exercise is vital to reducing your body fat to optimum levels.

When you put Clarence's formula together, what you get is this: High-Fiber Diet + Weight Training + Aerobics = A Lean Body!

Yes, I know, many people who want to lose weight virtually shudder and cringe at the very mention of the word "exercise" (and some diet promoters, of course, take advantage of this fear by advertising that you can lose such-and-such number of pounds *without exercise* — as if exercise were some sort of dread penalty). Fortunately, the large number of people — men and women, young and old, average citizens, rather than athletes — who are now exercising is proof that the public aversion to exercise is a fast-fading phenomenon.

One reason why this aversion has diminished is that almost every sedentary person in America knows someone — a neighbor, a friend, a relative, a fellow worker, etc. — who exercises, and more often than not the exercising individual is neither an athlete nor a superman (or superwoman). So the message has begun to sink in: If Fred, or Sally, or Jane, or Tom, Dick and Harry are exercising and even enjoying it, how difficult can an exercise program be?

And, of course, that's the correct message. As Clarence Bass illustrates in this book, exercise does not need to be painful or even a chore. Certainly, you can make it that way if you want to, but in terms of the type of exercise program we're talking about here, no one is asking you to run a four-minute mile! Rather, exercise can be as gentle as walking around the block, because an effective exercise program can start with something that simple and gentle.

"The aproach to maintaining leanness has to be a lifestyle approach," Clarence says. "It has to be something you can be comfortable with at all times. And that's what I've done. I enjoy my diet. Even if health wasn't a factor, I wouldn't change it (the diet). And I enjoy my exercise program."

Dr. Arno (Arnie) Jensen, who supervised Clarence's physiology testing at The Cooper Clinic in Dallas, Tex., says, "A complex high-carbohydrate, high-fiber diet like Clarence eats (fruits, vegetables and grain products) is a great diet. You can eat all you want, and still maintain an excellent percent body fat if you have the proper exercise program."

Lean For Life is a unique book in many ways. Certainly, I do not know of any other book on weight loss that provides such a common-sense, logical, scientific approach to nutrition, along with a detailed, step-by-step, progressive exercise program involving *both* weight training and aerobics, along with such a sensitive, encouraging approach to motivation — how to stay with it

3

(whether we're talking about diet or exercise). It's also unique among weight-loss books in that Clarence Bass not only shows you how to become perpetually lean but, being a former Past-40 Mr. America champion bodybuilder, he also shows you how to develop a shapely, attractive and superbly fit body in the process. In short, no other book I know of "brings it all together" as completely and effectively as *Lean For Life.*

Whether you already exercise or are totally sedentary, this book has something for you. For example, by reading *Lean For Life,* bodybuilders can learn to add more aerobics to their exercise program; those who are serious runners, cyclists, etc., can learn to add weight training to their regimen. Perhaps most importantly of all, people who are couch potatoes can learn to roll off the couch and do something about it before they go to seed — pardon the pun, but you get the point!

Although the lifestyle approach presented here will be more of a transition for the sedentary individual than the active person, and therefore will require perhaps more of an effort (at least psychologically), it will also be a much greater benefit to the sedentary individual, because anyone who is sedentary is that much farther removed from the lifestyle or approach that keeps you perpetually lean and trim. If you fall in that category, take this opportunity to do something invaluable for yourself — start an exercise program. No matter how gentle or light the program, get started *now!* Sooner or later, you'll be glad that you did.

As you read *Lean For Life,* you'll find it's chock full of insights and information about nutrition, health, exercise and weight loss. Even if you don't choose to put every aspect of Clarence's approach into operation in your life, the education you'll receive in reading this book is well worth the time and effort.

One point I want to make in closing: I know from personal experience that most overweight people aren't in that condition because they eat *too much,* but because they follow the wrong lifestyle. In other words, there's something wrong with the equation in their lives when it comes to calories burned vs. calories ingested. How do I know this? Because for years I've watched sedentary friends who are overweight chastise themselves for eating too much, while I sat beside them looking slim and eating twice as much as they did (of course, it should be noted that I'm a long-distance runner).

So you could say I know from my own life experience that those people aren't eating "too much" (they're actually eating very little compared to someone like me). And, indeed, surveys have shown that overweight people actually eat *less* than people who are healthy, fit and trim, because people in the latter category have a better balance between calories burned as a result of an active lifestyle and calories consumed through diet.

Thus, it can be said that people are overweight because they are uninformed in the area of health and body maintenance. Being uninformed, they fall victim to various weight-loss fads and formulas that are one-sided, superficial and about as effective in correcting the body's true condition as slapping a new paint job on a car that's out of tune and in distress. Diet promoters who actually say or even imply that people can lose weight on their diet *without exercise* are preaching a message that's a disservice to the public. Such a diet approach is pointless and it's silly. Worse still, the thousands of people who have followed and continue to follow such diets remain deluded and frustrated in their quest for the holy grail of a lean, healthy, attractive body — the very body Clarence Bass shows you how to achieve easily, sensibly and permanently with his common-sense, self-motivating lifestyle approach.

Read his book, and you won't be uninformed anymore. Moreover, follow his approach, and you'll be — as he promises — lean for life!

David Prokop
Los Angeles, Calif.
Dec. 8, 1991

CHAPTER I

LIFESTYLE CHANGE: THE APPROACH THAT WORKS

Photo by Guy Appelman

CHAPTER I
LIFESTYLE CHANGE: THE APPROACH THAT WORKS

SOLUTION FOR AMERICA'S OBSESSION

According to a recent cover story in *U.S. News & World Report,* getting slim is America's obsession. Turmoil in the Soviet Union, events in the Middle East and the state of the economy fill the news; still, as the magazine puts it, "what people really care about is losing weight." There's a problem, however. Fat-loss expert and humorist Covert Bailey put his finger on it when he quipped in his book *Fit or Fat?* (Houghton Mifflin, 1977): "The American public has been dieting for 25 years — and has gained five pounds." Unfortunately, that's not only funny, it's also true.

A few years back, the public television program *Nova* presented an episode called "Fat Chance in a Thin World." Frankly, it was pretty depressing. The basic message was that diets don't work: 95% of those who lose weight by dieting gain it back within one year! By mid-life, more than half of Americans are overweight. What's more, *Nova* said, it's getting worse: In the past 15 years, the weight of the average American adult has increased by five pounds. So, you see, Covert Bailey probably had his tongue firmly embedded in his cheek when he made that comment, but what he said was no joke.

> *"The bottom line is that most people can, with a combination of psychology, changes in eating habits and exercise, lose weight and keep it off."*—U.S. News and World Report

Still, there's hope. We're finally getting a handle on how to lose fat and keep it off. Crash diets are on the way out. "Reshape-your-body-in-a-month" programs are being replaced by an emphasis on healthy lifestyle changes in eating and exercise. The editors of *U.S. News & World Report* are correct: "The bottom line is that most people can, with a combination of psychology, changes in eating habits and exercise, lose weight and keep it off."

Now let's look at some of the reasons why past weight loss efforts have failed.

STARVATION DIETS BACKFIRE

Ironically, many dieters fail because they don't eat enough. They skip meals and starve themselves. They try to rely on will-power, and it just doesn't work. Severe calorie restriction almost always leads to failure.

Geneen Roth explained why in her fascinating book about compulsive eating, *Feeding the Hungry Heart* (The Bobbs-Merrill Company, 1982). Roth says that diets don't work because they're based on deprivation. She maintains: "A binge is the other side of a diet; it is built into it; it is inevitable. For every diet there is an equal and opposite binge."

A recent article in *The New York Times* about dieters and their cravings gave several hard-hitting examples of what it describes as "the fast-and-binge roller coaster." The one I like best is bizarre, but it illustrates the intense psychological pressure that can build up during the course of a severe diet. It drives home Geneen Roth's point dramatically.

The story concerns a 47-year-old Manhattan lawyer who had lost 143 pounds on a liquid formula diet. After a time, he started dreaming about food, and finally closed his office door one Friday, drew up an itinerary and hired a car and driver for the next day. According to *The Times,* from noon to 7:30 P.M. the next day, he sat in the back seat... eating! After 22 stops, there he was, surrounded by wrappers and carry-out food containers, having consumed thousands of calories. He ended up gaining 21 pounds in 13 days!

This poor man's plight shows that severe diets almost always fail. The truth is that no diet based on denial and deprivation works for very long.

Geneen Roth recommends that we forget about dieting and instead start listening to our bodies. She claims that with practice your body will tell you what and when to eat and, most importantly, when to stop. Roth is on the right track. I'll have a lot to say about that later. First, however, it's important that we understand as much as we can about why diets don't work.

YO-YO DIET FRUSTRATIONS

Many dieters fall victim to the yo-yo syndrome. They lose weight, all right, but they regain all they lost — and often more! They cycle up and down many times over the course of a lifetime. This is terribly frustrating, of course, but that's only part of the difficulty. Unfortunately, with every up-and-down cycle, their weight problem gets worse. That's because research has shown that repeated cycles of weight loss and gain make later weight-loss attempts more difficult, and the weight is regained more rapidly.

In a study with laboratory rats, Kelly Brownell, Ph.D., a professor of psychiatry at the University of Pennsylvania School of Medicine, observed that after the animals regained the weight they had lost when they were placed on a diet, it took more than *twice as long* to lose it the second time around, even though they were fed the same number of calories. The problem at the other end is that it took less than one-third the time to gain all the weight back compared to the first up-and-down cycle.

Specifically, the animals lost their excess weight in 21 days on the first try, but it took 46 days to shed the extra weight a second time. It took them 45 days to regain the weight the first time, and only 14 days to put it on again the second time.

It works the same way with people. Brownell has found that amateur wrestlers who lose and gain weight repeatedly have significantly lower metabolic rates than wrestlers who maintain a constant weight. Apparently, the body responds to repeated efforts at weight loss by automatically lowering its metabolic rate to conserve scarce calories. It's our built-in survival mechanism. The body perceives dieting as life-threatening starvation. In addition, it produces more of the enzymes responsible for the depositing of fat. That's why the fat goes back on so fast when eating is resumed.

There's also another process at work, especially if a starvation diet is used and loss is rapid. The additional problem is that the weight loss is not all fat. Considerable lean tissue is lost as well. That's a serious drawback, because most of the food we eat is burned by our muscles. Losing muscle means we burn fewer calories (i.e., our rate of metabolism slows down). Consequently, when the dieter starts eating again, fat is gained even faster than before because there's less muscle to burn calories from hour to hour each day. To compound the problem, the lean tissue lost is usually replaced with fat when the weight is regained. In short, with each up-and-down cycle, the person ends up with a greater percentage of body fat than before!

Exercise physiologist and nutrition counselor Linda Crockett, writing in *The Runner* magazine (later incorporated into *Runner's World*), presented a case history that demonstrates the devastating results of the yo-yo syndrome. A female runner whose body weight was normal based on height/weight charts complained of "a general lack of vigor." Underwater weighing revealed that she had a body fat of 46% — no wonder she felt listless! She was carrying 63.5 pounds of fat on what appeared to be a normal 138-pound body. Her background explains how she came to be so fat.

At the age of 29, she had been dieting half her life, including two days of total fasting every week of the preceding year. She claimed to eat normally on the other days, but Crockett reported that she actually binged on high-fat foods, particularly ice cream. Explained Crockett, "The woman lost both muscle and fat when she fasted, but gained mostly fat during her binge-eating periods."

THE COMFORT FACTOR

What's the main reason why people can lose weight, but they can't keep it off? Dr. Maria Simonson, director of the Health, Weight and Stress Program at Johns Hopkins University and author of *The Complete University Medical Diet* (Warner Books, 1983), calls this "the old bugaboo." She has observed, "Staying thin is harder than getting thin. The reason is that we are willing to restrict ourselves for a certain length of time but not, heaven forbid, forever."

Obviously, what's needed is a fat-loss/weight-maintenance program we can be comfortable with *forever*.

In fact, that's the answer to permanent fat loss: Call it "the comfort factor." If you're comfortable with your diet and exercise program, you'll be happy to stay with it . . . yes, forever. *U.S. News & World Report* phrased it like this: "The human body can be made to give up its extra pounds of flesh, but the tactics employed must be those of the blandisher, not the bully." In other words, strong-arm tactics don't work. To rid your body of excess fat once and for all, you must coax, cajole and ease — never force — the fat off.

As you read on, I'll tell you how I do that, and how you can, too. We'll explain how to adopt a comfortable, healthy lifestyle that will make and keep you lean for life.

CHAPTER II

MOTIVATION: KEY TO SUCCESS

Enjoy the process. *Photo by Chris Lund.*

CHAPTER II
MOTIVATION: KEY TO SUCCESS

LET'S MAKE A DEAL

You're motivated, obviously; otherwise you wouldn't be reading this book. You're probably already on a diet of some sort and following an exercise program as well. You may be a bodybuilder seeking to increase your aerobics to become leaner and fitter. Perhaps you're a runner or cyclist interested in balancing your program with strength training. Maybe diet is your nemesis; you've tried dieting and it hasn't worked for you. Although this book assumes some prior exposure to exercise, you may even be a couch potato with a built-in bias against exercise and the waistline to show for it. For whatever reason, you desire to change and improve yourself. You want to be lean for life. So, definitely, you are motivated.

Actually, as suggested by the fast-and-binge roller coaster we talked about in Chapter I, the problem many people have is too much motivation, rather than too little. People willing to starve themselves to lose weight don't lack motivation. No, the real problem is that their motivation is misdirected.

Odd as it may seem, many people are so motivated, so determined, that they defeat themselves. They burn out and give up. Like our Manhattan lawyer, their diet turns into a binge. It works the same with exercise. Overly strenuous and oppressive workout regimens soon give way to sedentary living.

I can almost guarantee that this won't happen if you follow the progress-oriented, comfortable, lifestyle approach we'll be discussing here. It's a common-sense approach that keeps you motivated.

You should know up front, however, that it's not a passive approach. It will take effort and study on your part. We'll spend a lot of time going over the reasons why things work — or don't work. You may even gain a little weight sitting around reading the detailed information on diet and exercise (especially exercise) you'll find in this book. (That happened to me when I was writing my book *Ripped 2*. I gained fat telling people how to lose fat. Funny, but true.)

I promise you this: Stick with me to the end, and you'll be well rewarded. The more you learn about the Lean-For-Life approach, the better it will work for you. Think of it this way: It took me a lifetime to accumulate the information you're going to get in the few days it will take you to read this book. And that's just the beginning, because if you follow my advice you'll almost surely be rewarded with a lifetime of leanness — and the fitness and health that comes in the bargain. Do we have a deal? Good. Let's get started.

THE PROBLEM: STAYING WITH IT

For most people, the problem is staying motivated. Just about everyone has been fired up at one time or another to go on a diet and start exercising. Determined to lose weight, we start off filled with enthusiasm for the task of "getting in shape." Regretfully, the barbells gathering dust under our beds, the cobwebs streaming from the stationary bikes in our garages, and the too-tight-to-fit clothes hanging in the back of our closets attest to the fact that interest soon wanes. Before long we're back doing all the things that got us "out of shape" in the first place. Our old habits soon regain the upper hand.

Clearly, motivation is a key element in the lifestyle approach to fitness. To stay lean for life we must stay motivated... yes, forever. But, take it from me, that's a lot more practical and do-able than you might think.

I should know. I've been training for about 40 years now. I picked up a barbell for the first time when I was barely into my teens, and I've been watching my diet and exercising ever since. In many ways, I'm more fit now in my 50s than I've ever been before.

Needless to say, the years have taught me a lot about staying motivated. And in these pages we'll talk about ways and means to help you stick with it through thick and thin. I'm going to tell you about many of the things that have motivated me over the years. Why? Because that will help you analyze your own motivation. And that's important. A true understanding of the factors that put steam in your personal boiler, so to speak, will help you keep the fire burning bright.

Motivation, of course, is a many-faceted thing. As my own experience will show, our motivation changes over time. Some of the factors that have motivated me, I know, may not be important to you. For example, I realize that the first factors we'll discuss, all of them health related, are not the primary motivation for most people. Still, at certain times, they're important for many people. If

16

increasing your longevity and preventing coronary artery disease, diabetes and hypertension don't interest you, then I suggest you skip to the section titled "The Master Passion." It discusses self-esteem, which is of interest to just about everyone.

Don't skip a word after that, however. The last two sections, "New Horizons" and "Formula For Success," are crucial to your understanding of the Lean-For-Life program. In later chapters, we'll repeatedly refer back to the principles discussed there.

Now let's look at the health benefits of staying lean and fit. Most doctors will tell you that you can do more — a lot more — to keep yourself healthy than they can do for you. My friend, Dr. Arnie Jensen, a preventive medicine specialist at the famous Cooper Clinic in Dallas, Texas, puts it this way: "Health is 50% lifestyle, 10% medicine and the rest is genetics and luck."

That's exciting and motivational, especially if, like me, you're over 50.

"Health is 50% lifestyle, 10% medicine and the rest is genetics and luck," says Dr. Arnie Jensen (shown here). *Photo by Justin Joseph.*

HEALTH BENEFITS OF FITNESS AND FAT LOSS

As a teenager, health was near the bottom of my list of reasons for starting to lift weights. Actually, if I considered the health benefits of exercise at all, it was little more than a passing thought. Like any young kid, my motivation was simply to get strong and muscular in order to improve my athletic performance and impress my friends.

It wasn't long, however, before I discovered *Strength & Health* magazine. Like *Muscle & Fitness* today, *Strength & Health* was the leading muscle magazine of its time. Bob Hoffman, the editor and publisher, was the United States Olympic weightlifting coach and a pioneer in the health-through-fitness field. He was also one of the first individuals in the food supplement business. His articles were my first real exposure to the idea that eating right was an important part of muscle building. Sure, my parents, like all parents, had told me to drink my milk and clean my plate so I'd grow up to be big and strong. But my first detailed information on vitamins, minerals, protein and so on came from Bob Hoffman.

I've come to discover that the benefits of becoming lean and strong extend far beyond being able to lift big weights and looking good in swimming trunks. *Photo by Guy Appelman.*

Clearly, Hoffman got through to me, because I remember taking a high school home economics course in nutrition. In fact, I was so eager to learn about good nutrition that I didn't mind being the only male in the class. Yes, I guess I was willing to do just about anything in those days that might help me get bigger and stronger.

Thinking back, I realize that *Strength & Health* and that high school nutrition course marked the beginning of my lifelong study of muscle and fitness, and their relationship to health. It's telling, I think, that of all my high school textbooks, the only one I still have is the one from that nutrition class.

Over the years my main priority has remained getting stronger and more muscular, but experience and study have convinced me that the best way to achieve those goals is also the best way to stay healthy. I've come to discover that the benefits of becoming lean and strong extend far beyond being able to lift big weights and looking good in swimming trunks. In fact, the evidence is so clear that even a hard case like me is forced to admit that part of my motivation comes from a desire to stay healthy.

Let me give you some health facts that I find especially compelling; they help me stay enthusiastic about eating right and exercising regularly. My bet is that they'll whet your appetite for the lean lifestyle as well.

A LITTLE FITNESS GOES A LONG WAY

The results of a remarkable study published recently in *The Journal of the American Medical Association* should get even confirmed couch potatoes on their feet. This research, conducted by the Institute for Aerobics Research in Dallas, demonstrates that you don't have to spend hours in the gym or on the track to derive worthwhile benefits. Even a minimal amount of exercise — a brisk 30-45 minute walk each day is enough — protects you against premature death. As I said earlier, you don't have to bully yourself. A little fitness goes a long way.

The Institute for Aerobics Research, an offshoot of The Cooper Clinic, studied 10,224 men and 3,120 women who were given a preventive medical examination, including a maximal treadmill test, between 1970 and 1981. After their exam, these 13,344 men and women were followed for an average of more than eight years. At the end of that time, 240 men and 43 women, all of whom were in good health when examined, had died. The subjects were placed in five fitness categories based on their treadmill performance. The 20% with the

People who exercise even moderately tend to live longer.

lowest treadmill times were classified as unfit, the top 20% were classified as highly fit, and those in the three middle categories were classified as moderately fit.

Through statistical analysis, the researchers found that men in the first group, the least fit, had a mortality rate 3.44 times greater than the most fit men. The least fit women had a mortality rate 4.65 times greater than those in the best shape.

Common sense says that fit people should live longer than couch potatoes. This study proves it. Even after weeding out other risk factors, including smoking, age, cholesterol level, weight, blood pressure and family history of heart disease, researchers found that deaths were sharply higher in the least-fit category than in the moderately-fit groups — more than double for men and almost twice as high for women.

But, significantly, those in the high-fitness group were only slightly less likely to die than those in the medium-fitness groups. In other words, you don't have to be superfit to greatly reduce your chances of dying prematurely. Even moderate fitness affords significant protection, not only from cardiovascular disease and cancers, but also against death from a wide variety of other causes. Simply put, people who exercise even moderately tend to live longer.

This proves the value of doing even a little exercise; it should get sedentary folks everywhere thinking — and exercising. I know it helps me stay motivated. How about you?

Now let's turn to another study, this time mainly involving diet, which was conducted recently.

DIET CHANGE OPENS CLOGGED ARTERIES

Arterial blockage is normally considered a problem that can't get better; it can only get worse. But a study recently published in the British medical journal *Lancet* shows that mild exercise and a careful diet, without drugs, can not only halt heart disease but actually reverse it.

The Lifestyle Heart Trial directed by Dean Ornish, M.D., head of the Preventive Medicine Research Institute, Sausalito, Calif., and a faculty member at the University of California San Francisco School of Medicine, is an ongoing study to determine whether lifestyle changes alone — no drugs, no surgery — can not only slow or stop the progress of heart disease, but actually open clogged arteries. The study produced the first hard evidence that the answer is yes.

Forty-eight patients with documented coronary artery disease (computer enhanced X-ray showed that their heart arteries were partially blocked) were divided into experimental and control groups. Significantly, all of these people were already restricting fat intake to 30% as usually recommended for heart disease patients. The patients (28) in the experimental group were put on an extremely low-fat diet (10%) plus minimal exercise and stress management. The remaining 20 patients, the control group, were not asked to make lifestyle changes.

The diet followed by the experimental group included fruits, vegetables, grains, legumes and soybean products. There were no calorie restrictions. No animal products were allowed except egg whites and non-fat milk or yogurt. Approximately 10% of the calories in the diet came from fat, as mentioned, and, in addition, about 20% came from protein and 70% from predominantly complex carbohydrates.

As you'll soon see, that's very much like the Lean-For-Life diet we recommend. In our diet, however, some adjustments are made to enhance flavor and eating pleasure, because we want the diet to be comfortable, an eating program you'll be happy to stick with all your life.

In the Lifestyle Heart Trial, the experimental group was also asked to exercise (usually walking) for a minimum of three hours per week — 30 minutes per session at 50-80% of the age-adjusted maximum heart rate. In other words, this group was put on a mild exercise regimen.

After one year on the program, the coronary arteries of all patients were again examined by computer enhanced X-ray to determine what changes, if any, had occurred.

Lifestyle changes may not only keep your coronary arteries clean and open, but actually reverse blockage in only one year!

Dr. Ornish and his associates found that 82% of those on the extremely low-fat diet showed an improvement in their coronary blood vessels. The average degree of clogging dropped from 60% to 56%. In the control group (the people who were not asked to make any lifestyle changes), the degree of clogging *rose* from 62% to 64%. Importantly, patients on the low-fat diet reported a 91% drop in heart pain, generally within a few weeks. In contrast, control-group patients reported a 165% rise in heart pain frequency.

These changes in blockage may seem small, but they're actually very impressive when you consider that coronary blockage occurs over a period of decades. According to Dr. Ornish, one would not expect to find large changes in only one year. Plus, even a small amount of widening in clogged arteries has a large practical effect. This is demonstrated by the very significant reduction in heart pain seen in the experimental group (the people on the low-fat diet) as contrasted to the increased angina experienced in the control group.

Remember too that, even before the experiment, both groups were already limiting their fat intake to 30% as recommended by the American Heart Association. Think about it: On a diet containing a relatively low percentage of fat (30%), coronary artery blockage increased. Now imagine what happens on the high-fat diet (40% or more) most Americans consume!

Yes, this is big news. It proves for the first time that lifestyle changes alone — things you can do for yourself without the help of a doctor — may not only keep your coronary arteries clean and open, but actually reverse blockage in only one year!

Dr. Ornish and his colleagues do not explain the precise mechanism by which the coronary arteries were opened. I don't think they know exactly. Nevertheless, it is no doubt significant that, in the experimental group, total cholesterol fell by 24.3% and LDL-cholesterol (the bad kind) fell by 37.4%. This is important because there's solid evidence that a high cholesterol level significantly increases a person's risk of heart attack.

The report in *The Lancet* also does not reveal whether the experimental group experienced a reduction in body fat level. It's a good bet that this did occur, however, because an extremely low-fat diet, even without calorie restriction, combined with exercise almost invariably results in fat loss.

Of course, one of the most important reasons to lose body fat is to avoid cholesterol deposits in the arteries. As Lawrence E. Lamb, M.D., states in his book *The Weighting Game* (Lyle Stuart, 1988), "Eliminating excess body fat is often one of the very best ways to lower the total cholesterol level."

So, you see, appearance is only one reason to lose body fat, and maybe not even the most important reason at that. Lifestyle change, diet and exercise will reduce your body fat and improve your appearance, but in the bargain you get the longevity benefits of lower cholesterol and unclogged arteries as well.

Encouraging? I think so.

CLOSER TO HOME: DIABETES AND STROKE

This topic has special meaning for me. My father had adult onset diabetes and died from a stroke. So I may have a genetic predisposition to develop similar problems. In fact, at the conclusion of my evaluation at The Cooper Clinic a few years ago, Dr. Arnie Jensen gave me sobering yet encouraging news. He said, "I suspect that if you were not careful with your weight, diet and exercise program that you most likely would develop adult onset diabetes." His assessment was based on my family history and the finding that my blood glucose and triglycerides were slightly elevated.

In my book *The Lean Advantage 2,* I discussed diabetes at length, so I won't go into detail here. But I do want to emphasize again, briefly, the role of leanness and lifestyle in controlling diabetes. I'd also like to say a few words about preventing high blood pressure and stroke.

As little as a few extra pounds of body fat may increase the risk of developing diabetes, according to Lawrence E. Lamb, M.D. In *The Weighting Game,* Dr. Lamb illustrates the effect of diet and exercise on diabetes by recounting a fascinating study carried out by Dr. Kerin O'Dea of the Department of Medicine, University of Melbourne, Australia.

Dr. O'Dea studied 10 middle-aged Australian aborigines who returned to a hunter-gatherer lifestyle. They had previously followed a Western lifestyle, which included a diet high in fat and calories. Before the change, all were obese and diabetic. Of course, when they returned to the old ways, they ate only what they could hunt, fish or collect. Their diet averaged only 1200 calories a day and, as you can well imagine, their activity level increased greatly.

Dr. Lamb summarized the predictable result: "They all lost weight steadily and at two months their blood glucose level had fallen and their glucose tolerance was improved. By seven weeks... the triglycerides (fat) level in the blood had fallen to normal."

This study shows in a colorful way why Dr. Jensen was able to tell me reassuringly, "I do not anticipate that you will ever have any problems if you stay lean, fit and continue to eat smart as you are currently doing."

Lifestyle is equally important in preventing hypertension (high blood pressure). This relates to my father's death because, according to Kenneth H. Cooper, M.D., high blood pressure is the major causative factor for all forms of stroke.

The Harvard Medical School Health Letter reported recently that most people can lower their blood pressure by adjusting their lifestyle.

Hypertension is a disease of civilized life. The *Harvard Medical School Health Letter* reported recently that most people can lower their blood pressure by adjusting their lifestyle. Dr. Cooper confirms this in his book *Overcoming Hypertension* (Bantam Books, 1990). He gives this hopeful pronouncement: "I've discovered that exercise and a healthy diet and lifestyle can keep the average person's blood pressure near the levels of youth."

Specifically, Dr. Cooper says being overweight may be the primary factor contributing to hypertension and stroke. Losing all or most of your excess body fat will "often produce a dramatic improvement in blood pressure levels," adds Dr. Lamb in *The Weighting Game*. That's why diet and exercise are so important; they're the best way to lose body fat and keep it off.

As you probably already guessed, Dr. Jensen is also optimistic that I won't fall victim to a stroke like my dad. My lifestyle keeps my body fat *and* my blood pressure low. Dr. Jensen says my blood pressure readings are "absolutely superb."

So I've got good reason to be enthusiastic about diet and exercise. Hopefully, I've boosted your enthusiasm as well.

Because of my family history, I've got good reason to be enthusiastic about diet and exercise. Hopefully, I've boosted your enthusiasm as well. *Photo by Guy Appelman.*

THE MASTER PASSION

Dr. George Sheehan, probably today's foremost philosopher of fitness, has pointed out that there are many levels of motivation. Fitness converts are often motivated initially by fear. Their doctor warns: "If you don't start exercising and lose some weight, you're going to die before your time."

Our discussions thus far on the health benefits of fitness and fat loss have targeted that level of motivation. That's fine as far as it goes. Yes, the medical facts on fitness are truly compelling. The problem, as Dr. Sheehan has said, is that most people won't *continue* doing something just because it's good for them. Another level of motivation is necessary to keep them on track, something more immediate than what might happen years down the road.

The psychological rewards of exercise and proper diet often come into play at that point and recharge one's sagging zeal for fitness. That's because being lean and fit, in simple terms, makes one feel better emotionally. Among other things, it enhances your self-image. Dr. Edward D. Greenwood, a psychiatrist at the Menninger Clinic, stated it more formally: "Exercise promotes a sense of well-being by enhancing ego strength, dissipating anger and hostility, relieving boredom and resolving frustration." The words of Mark Twain, however, may express it best. Fitness feeds what Twain called "the Master Passion, the hunger for self approval." In short, being fit makes you feel good about yourself.

I know that firsthand. The psychological benefits of fitness have spurred my training for almost 40 years. I first enjoyed the emotional rewards as a teenager.

In *Ripped 2* I wrote: "Discovering at an early age that I could lift more weight than most other boys gave me self-confidence. It enhanced my self-image and helped me weather my adolescent years. My high school principal said I came to his school with the reputation of a delinquent and graduated a model student. Lifting had a lot to do with my transformation. It made me feel good about myself."

Not only does physical training make you look better, it gives you a sense of accomplishment. Nothing is more satisfying than to set a goal, work hard and accomplish it. I established that pattern in my youth and it has served me well ever since.

Once you experience the sense of well-being that comes from being strong and fit, as I did in my teens, you never want to go back. The die is cast. I knew I wouldn't like facing the world with atrophied muscles and a potbelly. And I never have. My training became an important part of the positive view I had — and have — of myself. It was part of what made — and makes — me feel that

"I'm okay."

My experience, of course, is not unique. Jan and Terry Todd, authors of *Lift Your Way to Youthful Fitness* (Little, Brown & Co., 1985), have found that physical training can make a dramatic difference in the way people, both young and old, feel about themselves.

First, they know personally what training does for one's self-esteem. Jan is one of the best-known female strength athletes of our time — she set a world record of 545 pounds in the squat lift. Her husband Terry was one of our first national power-lifting champions. In addition, they are keen observers and chroniclers of the physical culture scene, both past and present. Terry is a former editor of *Strength & Health,* the magazine which, as I mentioned before, influenced me as a youth. Jan and Terry now oversee the Todd-McLean Collection at the University of Texas at Austin, the most complete library of physical culture-related materials to be found anywhere. They also co-edit *Iron Game History,* a journal dedicated to the history of physical culture.

> **Research has shown that physical training can make a dramatic difference in the way people, both young and old, feel about themselves.**

Furthermore, as part of their work at the Physical Education Department at the University of Texas, where Jan is a researcher and Terry a professor, they studied the effect of weight training on self-concept. Their research projects, done in cooperation with Dr. James Hilyer of Auburn University, have demonstrated that weight training significantly improves self-image.

As an example, both before and after two weight-training research projects, one involving men and the other women, the Todds administered a self-image test to determine whether lifting affects the way their subjects perceived themselves. Both the men and women underwent significant positive changes in self-image. Interestingly, the women experienced greater improvement in self-image than the men.

Here's the glowing report of one female subject at the end of a 10-week training period: "The training has really changed the way I feel about myself. It's not just that I'm stronger or that my body is firmer and my skin clearer than it was in the past. It has somehow changed my whole attitude to life. I feel more confident, less afraid to try new things."

So, you see, one of the most important benefits of a healthy life-style is that it answers the need we all have for self-approval; it feeds our Master Passion. That powerful incentive has kept me training year after year.

It'll keep you motivated as well because, as George Sheehan

wrote in *Personal Best* (Rodale Press, 1989), "Becoming the best you can be makes you feel the best you can feel."

NEW HORIZONS

Another strong motivating force is inspiration. Like the need for self-approval, inspiration keeps us moving down the fitness track. It stimulates us to exceed ourselves, to strive to be the best we can be.

Unfortunately, we often underestimate our capabilities. As George Sheehan expressed it in *Personal Best,* "We sell ourselves short.... When our horizons narrow, our goals do also." He also said, "The problem in motivation is knowing what it is we could and must want to begin with." In short, we need something — an event, an experience, a revelation — or someone to open our eyes to that which is possible, to focus us on new horizons.

Kenny Moore, one of my favorite writers, reported not long ago in *Sports Illustrated* how an Olympic champion was inspired to raise her sights. After 15 years in athletics, Louise Ritter had achieved her dream by winning the Olympic gold medal for the high jump in Seoul, Korea. Still, Moore related, after returning home to Dallas she went through a period of despondency. "I couldn't figure out what was wrong," she said. "Everything I wanted happened, and I'm depressed?" Moore explained why: "Because a goal achieved is a goal lost." Obviously, she needed a new goal, a new horizon.

She found it when she received incontrovertible evidence that she was selling herself short. High-speed film taken at the U.S. Olympic Trials showed that she cleared 6'6¼" by enough to put her easily over a world record height of 6'11". Reviewing that film made her realize that on a good day under the right conditions she was capable of establishing a new world record. Presto! The cloud lifted. No more depression. She had an exciting new challenge. Her eyes were opened wide to the fact that a world record was within her reach. She was inspired!

We need something or someone to focus us on new horizons.

In a similar vein, we are often inspired to new heights by role models. I've had many over the years. The first was my father. He was a track-and-field champion during his schoolboy days. He excelled in the discus, broad jump, high jump and pole vault. He was practically a one-man track team. In fact, all by himself he placed second as a team in the New Mexico high school track-and-field championships. In college, he came within inches of the world record in the pole vault.

I wanted to be an athlete just like my dad. His medals were kept in the downstairs hall closet. I took them out time after time and fantasized about following in his footsteps. Those medals, the representations of my dad's athletic achievements, gave me the first push to improve myself physically.

I wasn't cut out to be a track-and-field athlete, however. My first attempts at pole vaulting resulted in a dislocated shoulder, and I soon moved on to other pursuits. Nevertheless, without the inspiration provided by my father, I might not have aspired to be an athlete at all.

Fortunately, I experienced greater success lifting my dad's weights. He had bought the weights for himself, but I moved them into my room when I was about 12 or 13 — I must have been in the sixth or seventh grade — and claimed them for my own. That marked the beginning of my lifelong love affair with weight training.

When I was a sophomore in high school, I found a new role model. I'll never forget the experience. An upper classman, Gordon Modrall — he lived across the street from me — was honored at a high school awards ceremony for winning the State High School Pentathlon Championship, a five-event contest consisting of push-ups, chin-ups, jump reach, bar vault and 300-yard shuttle run. Seeing Gordie get his award as the whole school applauded inspired me. I made up my mind that I'd win that award the next year — and I did.

In later years, many lifting and physique champions served as my role models, inspiring me to be the best Olympic lifter, and then the best bodybuilder that I could be. Even now, after almost 40 years of training, I'm still motivated by role models. Let me tell you about my latest inspiration.

She — yes, *she* — was a young woman rower I had seen in action at an indoor rowing competition held early in 1990. The competition was sponsored by the Rocky Mountain Rowing Club and held at Denver's Cherry Creek Athletic Club. I had trained hard for the event and planned to set a new personal record for 2500 meters on the Concept II rowing machine. I thought I was a pretty good rower. In the Concept II world ranking, I had placed 66th out of 154 men in the 50-59 age category. Among the 30 competitors weighing less than 165 pounds, the lightweights, I ranked 11th.

Well, I did set a new personal record for 2500 meters in the competition, but I didn't win. In fact, I didn't even come close. In spite of my personal record, I placed only seventh in the veterans' category. The winner in my age group did 9:03 versus my 9:46. He and a number of other competitors showed me what is possible and convinced me that I could do much better.

Nevertheless, as good as the men were, the performance that impressed me the most was by the young woman I mentioned earlier. I'm guessing that she weighed a little less than me. I don't remember her exact time, but it was under 9:30. She rowed with powerful strokes, long and even. She was terrific! More than anything else, seeing her performance convinced me that I was setting my sights too low, that I was underestimating myself.

I focused on this woman's performance because size has a lot to do with rowing ability. Almost all the best times are by big, tall people. That was true of the top over-50 rower in Denver; he outweighed me by about 50 pounds and was at least six inches taller. It didn't really bother me that his time was better than mine. But the woman's performance was another story. She had no height or weight advantage, yet she still beat my time by a substantial margin. That set off a bell in my head.

It was like the four-minute-mile barrier. Once Roger Bannister broke through, the floodgates opened. Runners all over the world came to believe they could run a four-minute mile, and they did. That woman rower did the same thing for me.

In my first rowing session upon returning home, I hit a level of performance that I would have considered over my head only a few days earlier. With the woman rower as my inspiration, I became convinced that I had sold myself short in Denver, and that I could surpass my personal record by a substantial margin. I decided to train for a few weeks at a faster pace, and then go for a new PR. And that's what I did. Three weeks later, I proudly sent Concept II, Inc. a spanking new PR for their world list — 9:32.1.

That was many months ago. The icing on the cake came a few weeks ago as I write this, when Concept II published the 1990 world rankings. The total number of competitors in the 50-59 age category doubled, increasing to 315 from 154. I was 95th overall, which moved me from the middle third in 1989 to the top third in 1990. Among competitors weighing less than 165, I moved into the upper 25%!

I felt good about my new ranking — so good, in fact, that I immediately began thinking about doing even better in 1991.

So the message is this: Keep your eyes on the hills. Keep looking for new and broader horizons, and you'll find the inspiration necessary to become better than you think you can be. The professional motivator types generally leave me cold, but I'm convinced they're onto something when they proclaim: "If you can conceive it, you can achieve it." Because it's true — when you're inspired to think you can, you probably can.

When you're inspired to think you can, you probably can. *Photo by Chris Lund.*

FORMULA FOR SUCCESS

If there's one word that embodies the formula for success in training, it's enjoyment. Surprised? Probably so, because most people associate diet and exercise with suffering. You know the old saying, "No pain, no gain." When you think about it, however, you realize that's a formula for failure. It's human nature that a person won't keep doing something he or she doesn't enjoy.

That's not to say that productive exercise is always easy. On the contrary; it's often brutally hard. Discipline and willpower is necessary.

But in order for training to be successful, it must be enjoyable. It's simple common sense: If you enjoy an activity, you're likely to stay with it. If you don't enjoy something, you'll probably decide it's not worth the effort and stop doing it.

More specifically, if you find satisfaction and happiness in the process of training, you'll very likely continue exercising regularly and eating properly. What's more, you'll probably be more successful than you think you can be. Best of all, the combination of enjoyment and success will motivate you to make training a permanent part of your lifestyle.

The question, then, becomes: What makes training enjoyable? Fortunately, my training has been enjoyable and successful almost from the very beginning. It wasn't until years later, however, when I started writing, that I sat down and carefully analyzed why this was the case.

The results of that soul-searching are expressed in my book *The Lean Advantage,* where I wrote, "I've found that I'm happiest when I'm working hard to achieve some goal. I enjoy the process of moving closer and closer to the goal of peak condition. The process of losing fat and gaining muscle... is gratifying in and of itself."

That is not a new idea. As Mihaly Csikszentmihalyi (let's just call him "Dr. C"), a professor and former chairman of the Department of Psychology at the University of Chicago, relates in his insightful book *Flow: The Psychology of Optimal Experience* (Harper & Row, 1990), since the days of Aristotle it has been known that "periods of struggling to overcome challenges are what people find to be the most enjoyable times of their lives." In other words, enjoyment comes from laboring, slowly but surely, to succeed at some challenging task. That's basically the idea I expressed in my book.

It boils down to this simple proposition: Success breeds success. To stay motivated and enjoy your training, you must be successful. The reverse is also true, however. In order to be successful, you must stay motivated and enjoy your training. Sounds like a Catch-22, I know, but trust me, it's really not. Training, like most other activities, can be planned in a way that virtually guarantees success and enjoyment. Dr. C. explains how in *Flow*.

"Flow" is the term he uses to describe those times when people report feelings of concentration and deep involvement, or a genuinely enjoyable state of consciousness. Paraphrasing Dr. C., here's the blueprint followed by people who experience flow: They set appropriate goals, closely monitor feedback, and when they reach their goal, they up the ante, setting increasingly complex challenges for themselves.

Let's explore the flow formula in the context of training. "A fitness program without a challenge is like an Army battalion without a war," George Sheehan wrote in *Runner's World* (May 1989). In other words, you need a goal to give meaning to your training. Otherwise, as Dr. Sheehan puts it, you "start to feel like Sisyphus forever pushing the stone, yet never arriving at a goal."

> **Probably more than anything else, positive feedback which indicates that you are moving towards your goal, makes the training process enjoyable.**

To illustrate the importance of having a goal, Dr. Sheehan talked about a friend who teaches a much-in-demand fitness course at a state university. The protocol is not unusual: lifting weights one day and jogging the next. The students rarely drop out of the class, however. The reason, Sheehan explains, is because it's a mountain-climbing course. The students are preparing to climb Oregon's Mt. Hood.

"The mountain transforms this fitness program into preparation for a new and challenging experience," says Dr. Sheehan. "It changes something boring into something quite exciting."

So, using Dr. Sheehan's metaphor, if you want to experience flow in your training, the first thing you must do is "put a mountain at the end of your program."

The mountain, however, must be one you can reasonably expect to climb. To comply with the flow formula, your goal must be "appropriate." You must set realistic and achievable goals. That's because the strength of your motivation depends, in large part, on your success in reaching your goal. It does no good to set a pie-in-the-sky goal, like winning the Boston Marathon if you've just taken up jogging, or the Mr. Olympia title if you're a beginning bodybuilder. It's highly unlikely that you'll make meaningful progress toward such lofty goals.

Dieters often make this mistake. Extremely overweight people, in an initial burst of enthusiasm, vow to shed the excess weight in only a few weeks time. The predictable result is frustration and failure. By contrast, losing one pound per week is a goal most people can reasonably expect to achieve.

That, of course, brings us to feedback, the next element in the flow formula. Feedback is critical to motivation. Probably more than anything else, positive feedback which indicates that you are moving toward your goal makes the training process enjoyable. Remember, success breeds success.

That's another reason why the goal just mentioned — losing one pound per week — is a good example of the flow formula at work. Not only is that a realistic goal, it can be precisely monitored. The feedback is clear, immediate, and that's extremely satisfying.

Let me illustrate with a current experience. As I write this, I'm preparing to go to California to be photographed for *Muscle & Fitness* magazine (a meaningful goal, you'll note). I'm already quite lean, so I've decided to lose one-half pound of fat each week. To monitor my progress, I weigh myself and measure my waist each morning. I maintain a record of these measurements on a chart next to my bathroom scale.

When I checked myself this morning (it's Friday), I referred to the chart to see where I stood last Friday. I did this because the weekly trend is more important than the daily ups-and-downs which are bound to occur. I was pleased to see that I lost one and one-half pounds, plus I took half an inch off my waist. That's good, because the week before there was no change in either measurement. Fortunately, the trend is downward, and my progress is right on target.

Positive feedback like that keeps me motivated. You'll note I've chosen a comfortable rate of reduction. I'm not hungry and I don't feel at all deprived. By contrast, had I set out to lose five pounds a week, I'd certainly fall short and be miserable in the process. Believe me, starving yourself is not the way to become lean — or experience flow.

The final element of the flow formula is setting increasingly complex challenges for yourself. When you reach a goal, you must up the ante. A general principle, according to Dr. C., is that any activity can become enjoyable if you "take control of it, and cultivate it in the direction of greater complexity."

Without realizing it, I've actually followed the flow formula right from the start in my training. Thinking back, I now realize that this has been a critical factor in my training longevity. I've constantly set and achieved ever more challenging goals for myself. My book *Ripped 2* tells in detail how I moved from one realistic goal to the next, so I'll merely summarize here.

Like other beginners, my body responded well to my initial

training efforts. Inspired by my father, my first goal was to be as strong as my friends. After I achieved that goal, I trained for and won the State High School Pentathlon Championship. I went on from there to win city, state and regional weightlifting championships. When I reached my late 30s, I turned to bodybuilding where I was also successful, winning my class in the Past-40 Mr. America and Past-40 Mr. USA competitions.

Note that my first goal was to become as strong as my friends, not to become a world champion weightlifter or a Mr. America. I moved to more challenging goals, but only after I was successful at lower levels. I continually upped the ante, but I did it slowly and progressively. I didn't bite off more than I could chew. Again, without knowing it, I was following the flow formula.

As you've probably realized by now, my recent excursion into

Indoor-rowing competition gave me a challenging new mountain to climb. Here I am at the start of the Mile-High Indoor Rowing Classic held on February 2, 1991, in Denver, Colorado. I placed second in my age group. *Photo by Carol Bass.*

indoor-rowing competition was another example of the flow formula in operation. I had just begun casual and not-too-enthusiastic training when an entry form for the 1990 competition came in the mail. I said to myself, "This is just what I need! Competition to push me to a new personal record." As Dr. Sheehan would say, that gave me a challenging new mountain to climb.

You'll note that my goal was not to win the competition outright. I didn't set out to beat the other competitors. That would not have been realistic. I didn't know the other rowers nor their rowing times. And, frankly, I didn't much care. I long ago learned that the only competitor that really matters is me. I had no control over the other rowers. But I did know this: If I trained hard, I could probably set a new PR. For me, that was an appropriate goal, one which would practically guarantee positive feedback. In short, I structured my training for success. That approach allowed me to be satisfied with my efforts even though I only placed seventh.

What's more, seeing the other rowers in action, especially the female rower, provided me with a realistic basis to up the ante and set a more complex challenge for myself. I had no realistic basis to think I could equal or beat the rowing times of the bigger and taller men. The performance of that young woman, however, was another story. She was about my size. She gave me reason to raise my sights. She inspired me to go for still another PR, and a higher placing on the Concept II world list. As you know, that's exactly what I did. The flow formula worked again. Success breeds success.

So there you have it, the formula for success: Goals, Feedback and Challenge. Keep that blueprint in mind as we further explore the lifestyle approach that will make you lean for life. And always remember that the key is: Enjoy the process.

CHAPTER III

WHY A THREE-PRONGED APPROACH?

Photo by Chris Lund.

CHAPTER III
WHY A THREE-PRONGED APPROACH?

KNOWING WHY MAKES IT HAPPEN

The *Ziggy* cartoon in our local paper this morning made me chuckle. Ziggy, sort of a "poor soul" or "born loser" type of guy, is pointing away and leaning over in a determined posture while saying to his dog, who is stubbornly planted on his hindquarters: "Never mind *why,* just go fetch the stick!"

I found that especially amusing, because I identified with the dog. My father used to say, "The person who knows *how* works for the person who knows *why.*" I guess I took that to heart, because my mother used to get mad at me for asking so many questions. I believe she thought, like Ziggy, that her authority was being questioned. I don't know about Ziggy's dog, but that wasn't true in my case. I sincerely wanted to know why things were so. I still do.

As a lawyer, I always look for the reason behind a law; what is the legislature or the court trying to accomplish. Understanding why a law was made, of course, makes it easier to apply the law properly to a client's case. I approach fitness the same way. I want to know the why's and wherefore's behind every diet and training program. As in my legal work, that allows me to decide whether the program can be applied to good effect in my case.

Many people have a general idea which foods are healthy and which are not, and that if they eat less they'll lose weight. They know that running will improve their endurance and probably help them lose weight as well. They know that people who lift weights tend to be more muscular and stronger than those who don't.

But people usually don't know much beyond the generalities, however. They diet haphazardly, run a little bit and try to pump iron like the bodybuilders they see in the gym, and then they hope that something good will happen to their body. Worse still, they expect it to happen overnight.

Well, a regimen like that probably will bring about some desirable changes. But if you want maximum benefits in minimum time, however, you need to know the precise role diet, aerobics and weight training play in a fat-loss program. When I give a seminar, before I accept questions from the audience, I usually spend about 20 minutes explaining the "why" of each of these elements. That lays the groundwork for the audience to better understand the remainder of my talk, the nuts and bolts part, so to speak. Even more importantly, it equips each person to take what I say and mold it to fit his or her special and unique needs.

That's the purpose of this chapter: to help readers understand and apply the nutrition and exercise programs which follow.

THE ROLE OF DIET

As discussed in Chapter I, low-calorie diets are not an effective way to lose fat and keep it off. Severe calorie restriciton almost always leads to failure. It causes hunger and feelings of deprivation. You become unhappy, and that soon leads to bingeing. You gain back all the weight you lose, and probably more. In addition, your metabolic rate slows and you produce more of the enzymes responsible for the depositing of fat on the body. So when you start eating normally again, fat gain is even faster than before. What's more, since much of the weight you lost while on the restricted diet was muscle, it means you now have less muscle mass and, therefore, a lower calorie-burning capacity. The bottom line is that severe dietary restriction simply does not work.

Oprah Winfrey is a good example of the futility of going on a very low-calorie diet. As I'm sure many of you know, she lost 67 pounds in just a few months on a liquid formula diet, and then gained weight again — she won't say how much. "I'll never diet again," she told her talk show audience. Hopefully, the viewers who were so excited by her initial success got the important message that extreme diets are usually a disaster — long term.

A well-designed diet should supply the body with all the required nutrients. It must also create a calorie deficit and at the same time make you feel full and satisfied.

"The body can't shrink its fat cells and readjust its metabolism that fast," said George Blackburn, M.D., Ph.D., chief of the Nutrition/Metabolism Laboratory at the New England Deaconess Hospital (ironically, he also acts as a consultant to Ms. Winfrey's show on issues of obesity and health).

The propensity to regain the weight you lose that fast is three times as high as when it's lost more slowly, explained Dr. Blackburn, whose comments appeared in the *Tufts University Diet & Nutrition Letter.*

So what is the proper role of diet in a program to become lean and stay that way? First and foremost, a well-designed diet should supply the body with all of the required nutrients: carbo-hydrates, protein, fat, vitamins and minerals. It must also create a calorie deficit and — here's the tricky part — at the same time make you feel full and satisfied. The diet I follow and describe in detail in this book fills that bill perfectly.

That was the conclusion reached by The Cooper Clinic in Dallas during my medical and fitness evaluation there in 1988. Here's the assessment of Cindy Kleckner, R.D., L.D., nutritionist at The Cooper Clinic: "I have only good things to say about your diet. It's not only healthy and nutritious, but it's realistic. A lot of people go off the deep end in their diet. They restrict themselves. And quite frankly, it even turns me off.

"But as I listened to you talk about your diet, I think you're working on getting all the main nutrients. You're not excessive in any of the things that caused people problems. I would put an A++ on your diet."

The Cooper Clinic even subjected my diet to a computerized nutritional analysis. Dr. Arnie Jensen, the preventive medicine specialist mentioned earlier, described the results as "excellent." He added, "It is interesting that all your micronutrients are okay. It is unusual to see this in a nutrient evaluation."

The fact that my diet passed muster at The Cooper Clinic was actually no accident. Some years before, I had learned the hard way that starving yourself can make you fatter! As I detailed in *Ripped 2,* on two different occasions, underwater weighing showed that I lost weight and *gained* fat on such a diet. Preparing for the Past-40 Mr. America contest in one case and for a photo session in another, I had cut my calories too much, and this caused my body fat to go up although my weight went down. I had also learned, firsthand, that a comfortable diet is the only kind a person will stick with over a long period of time. So, like so many others, I had to experience the down side of rapid weight loss to believe it.

Like Oprah Winfrey and me (in days past), most people are in a hurry to lose weight. They simply won't accept the fact that starv-ing yourself actually will make you fatter in the long run. At our office we get letters and telephone calls almost daily from people who are subjecting themselves to ultra-low-calorie diets in a mis-taken belief that that's the way to lose fat, fast. Let me give you a few more facts to persuade you that a less restricted diet (i.e., eating more) will make you leaner in the long run.

First, Dr. Blackburn pointed out that lower-calorie diets "don't speed up the rate of weight loss." For example, he explained, a 420-calorie diet brings about no more weight loss than an 800-calorie-a-day diet, "because the body will just slow its metabolism to adjust." So there's simply no evidence to support the concept that the stricter the fast, the faster the results.

Now let me illustrate how ridiculous it is to cut calories to even 800 a day — let alone half that number as some do — by telling you how many calories it takes to maintain one's body weight. A moderately active man burns 14 to 16 calories a day for each pound of body weight. An inactive man burns 12 to 14 calories per pound, while a very active man burns 16 to 18 calories. For example, a moderately active man weighing 165 pounds requires 2,475 calories (15 × 165 = 2,475) to maintain body weight. A person of that size who cuts calories to the 800-a-day level is creating a 67% calorie deficit. That's like trying to satisfy a $30 debt with a $10 bill. It just doesn't work. It's starvation, not a diet. And, as mentioned above, it doesn't even speed the weight loss process materially. Restriction of that kind simply makes the dieter miserable — tired, hungry, deprived and eventually malnourished — and inevitably this leads to failure.

Women, who naturally have less muscle and more fat than men, burn about 10 or 15% fewer calories. A moderately active woman weighing 130 pounds requires about 1,700 calories to maintain her weight (13 calories × 130 = 1,690). So, as the Oprah Winfrey case shows, 800 calories a day is far too low for most women as well.

If you are to be successful, *you must not rush the reducing process!* Again, don't restrict your calorie intake too severely. Here's what I said in *Ripped 2* and repeated again in *Ripped 3*: "Don't try to lose more than one pound of fat a week. Reduce your calorie consumption *slightly*. Increase your calorie expenditure *slightly*." That's a formula worth repeating, because it's the formula for successful and permanent fat loss.

To give you a concrete example of how this works, I'll refer to myself. I weigh about 160 pounds, and I'm very active. Therefore, my predicted daily maintenance calorie level is approximately 2,720 (160 × 17). To lose one pound of fat (about 3,500 calories) in a week, I must create a daily calorie deficit of 500 calories (7 × 500 = 3,500).

The best way to accomplish this is to eat less *and* exercise more. I would only create half of the deficit, or 250 calories, through diet. That means I would bring my calorie intake down to 2,470 (2,720 less 250). Please note that's three times the number of calories that people on the 800-calorie diets consume. But I'll succeed, whereas they ultimately fail.

Part of the reason, of course, is exercise — aerobics and weights. Diet alone doesn't work. But a three-pronged approach made up of diet, aerobics and weights practically guarantees success. Diet

A three-pronged approach made up of diet, aerobics and weights practically guarantees success. *Photo by Allen Hughes.*

alone is a weak player, but when combined with aerobics and weights it becomes a steamroller. In the next two sections I'll explain why.

But first, so there's no misunderstanding, let me state again the proper role of diet in a program to become lean and stay that way. In addition to meeting the body's nutritional needs, a fat-loss diet should create a *slight* calorie deficit to burn off excess fat stores. At the same time — and this is critical — a properly designed diet must provide enough calories to make you feel full and satisfied. If you feel hungry and deprived, you're not eating enough. As we'll soon see, you're probably eating the wrong kind of food as well.

THE ROLE OF AEROBICS

In my early years of training I did very little aerobic exercise. Mainly I lifted weights. The only time I did endurance exercise was when there was no other choice. Even then, I didn't do much.

As mentioned earlier, the pentathlon event that I won in high school included a 300-yard shuttle run. That was my weakness. I didn't practice running as much as the other four events, and it showed. I also wrestled in high school. In fact, I placed second in the state meet. The coach made us run after practice to build endurance, but I wasn't enthusiastic about it. Again, it showed. The strength I built through weight training allowed me to dominate most opponents in the early minutes of a match, but my tongue was really hanging out, so to speak, at the end.

As I recall, I did little or no aerobic exercise during college and law school. My next encounter with endurance exercise came during basic training in the Air Force. And the main things I remember about that is blisters on my feet, and a big, fat sergeant calling me "Big Boy" and yelling, "Run faster." Needless to say, that experience didn't turn me on to aerobic exercise.

That came a few years later, right after I turned 30 and read Dr. Kenneth Cooper's runaway best-seller *Aerobics,* published in 1968. Through his revolutionary book, Dr. Cooper made me and millions of others around the world recognize the health benefits of aerobic exercise. That did it. I decided that in order to be really fit and healthy, I needed to do some aerobic exercise along with my weight training. So I started jogging on a more or less regular basis. I eventually joined the Albuquerque Roadrunners Club, a local group which held weekly fun-run competitions. I still have a handful of ribbons from those events, mostly third and fourth place, with a few seconds and even an occasional first in what was called the "Run For Your Life" category.

This photo shows my physique shortly before I read the book *Aerobics*. I was doing very little endurance exercise at the time, and it shows. I had plenty of muscle, but a good deal of fat as well. Look at those chubby cheeks! *Milner Studio photo.*

That was my first attempt at serious running. Competing against other men my age and fitness level, I finally got to the point where I could run a mile under six minutes. That's nothing, I realize, compared to top runners, but in my case it was quite an achievement. I trained hard all one summer to crack the six-minute barrier. Believe me, I was pleased with myself when I finally did it.

As I think back, that was the first time I achieved real satisfaction from an endurance event. As I had done many times before in weightlifting, I set a challenging goal for myself, worked hard, and then succeeded. As mentioned earlier, that's the formula that keeps a person motivated year after year. I kept running after that and added bike riding a short time later. Still, at that stage I didn't understand the key role aerobic exercise plays in the fat-loss process.

In 1977, as detailed in my book *Ripped,* when Dr. Ulrich C. Luft of Lovelace Medical Center first measured my body fat at 2.4%, I was still using basically a two-pronged approach: diet and weights. My only aerobic exercise at that time was a hard 20-mile bike ride once a week. That was the training plan I used in 1978 to win my class in the Past-40 Mr. America contest and, in 1979, when I won the Most Muscular Man Award at the Past-40 Mr. USA competition.

It wasn't until I read Covert Bailey's book *Fit Or Fat?* that I discovered the fat-loss magic in aerobic exercise. After that I gave aerobic exercise a more prominent place in my training. With further study and experience, my training eventually evolved to the point where I emphasized weights and aerobics equally. That's where I am today.

But what exactly is aerobic exercise? What are its health benefits? And what special role does it play in the fat-loss process?

Aerobic exercise is "exercise with oxygen," as distinguished from anaerobic exercise, "exercise without oxygen." Aerobic exercise conditions the heart, lungs and circulatory system to transport oxygen to the muscles more efficiently. It also conditions the muscles to use more oxygen. Importantly, fat can be burned as fuel only in the presence of oxygen, whereas glucose (sugar) can be burned without oxygen, that is anaerobically. We'll come back to the fat-burning aspects of aerobic exercise shortly.

Long-distance running is an example of aerobic exercise, while the 100-yard dash and weightlifting are examples of anaerobic exercise. The difference is mainly a matter of duration and intensity. Aerobic exercise is prolonged; it's easy enough so it can be continued for a long time. The breathing rate is higher than normal, but not so rapid that it can't be maintained.

By contrast, anaerobic exercise is short and intense; it's so hard that you can't keep doing it very long. Lactic acid builds up in the muscles — that happens when the oxygen requirement isn't being met — and you can't continue.

Aerobic exercise progresses on a pay-as-you-go basis; you breathe in the air you need and don't develop an oxygen debt. Anaerobic exercise creates an oxygen deficit which forces you to slow down or stop. I could talk about the various energy systems (immediate, short term and long term) but I've never found it helpful to think in those terms. (If you want that information, check out an exercise physiology book at your local library. The one I often use is *Exercise Physiology: Energy, Nutrition, and Human Performance* by William D. McArdle, Frank I. Katch and Victor L. Katch. The publisher is Lea & Febiger.)

For practical purposes, all one needs to know is that anything beyond a half-mile run is predominantly aerobic. As a rule of thumb, exercise below 80-85% of your maximum heart rate is aerobic; exercise that makes your heart beat faster than that is anaerobic. It's not really necessary to count your heart rate, however. Just remember that any pace you can continue for several minutes or more while maintaining a steady breathing rate is aerobic; it increases the efficiency of oxygen intake by the body and builds endurance.

The health benefits of aerobic exercise are many. As discussed in Chapter 2, The Cooper Clinic has proved, by measuring the aerobic fitness of thousands of men and women on the treadmill and then following them for almost a decade, that fit people tend to live longer. It's been well known for years, of course, that aerobic exercise protects against heart disease, lung disease, high blood pressure, diabetes and other lesser maladies.

In the course of writing this, I dug out my copy of *Aerobics* and reread Dr. Cooper's chapter on these clinical conditions. It's wonderful, inspiring reading. When I met Dr. Cooper in 1989 — I was on the treadmill in his office — the first thing I said was, "Your book got me started running more than 20 years ago." Needless to say, having the opportunity to tell him that in person was one of the high points of my second visit to The Cooper Clinic. If, like me, you need inspiration to begin regular aerobic exercise, I heartily recommend Dr. Cooper's classic text (or any of the many books he's written since then).

In *Aerobics,* Dr. Cooper didn't dwell on obesity but, without going into detail, he did say in no uncertain terms that aerobic exercise (plus diet) is the way to get rid of excess fat. My guess is that, at the time, he didn't know just how right he was. Let's turn to that now and fill in the details on the fat-loss benefits of aerobic

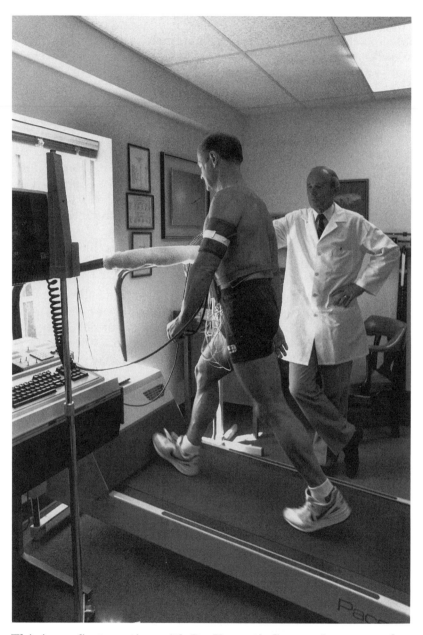

This is my first meeting with Dr. Kenneth Cooper. It was wonderful to have the opportunity to tell him in person that his book *Aerobics* got me started running more than 20 years ago. *Photo by Justin Joseph.*

exercise.

The first fat-loss benefit of aerobic exercise is just simple common sense, but it's extremely important to the long-term process of getting lean and staying lean. Regular aerobic exercise allows you to eat more; it takes the pressure off the diet side of the energy balance equation. That means you can lose fat and keep it off without hunger or the psychological stresses that inevitably go along with it.

Did you know that during exercise the energy requirements of skeletal muscles can increase 100 times? It's true. "Physical activity has by far the most profound effect on human energy expenditure," according to *Exercise Physiology,* the text mentioned earlier. That's why world-class endurance athletes nearly double their daily calorie expenditure as a result of three or four hours of hard training. In fact, according to the same textbook, most of us can generate energy expenditures that are 10 times resting levels during sustained "big muscle" exercise like running, rowing and cross-country skiing.

These are extremes, of course, provided here merely to demonstrate the calorie-burning potential or capacity of exercise. It's certainly not necessary to exercise three or four hours a day in order to become lean. Nor do you need to exercise with the intensity required to increase energy expenditure tenfold. As a matter of fact, simply walking on a daily basis makes a big difference over time. Let's see how this works.

A 154-pound person burns about 90 calories in walking one mile (heavier people burn more and those who are lighter less). About 30 of those calories, however, would be consumed even if the person was sitting still. So approximately 60 extra calories are expended in walking a mile. That's not many, I know, when you realize there are 3,500 calories in one pound of fat. Over the course of time, however, the extra calories mount up.

For example, I usually walk about 30 minutes after lunch and another 30 minutes in the evening. That's about three miles a day or 180 extra calories. Take out your pocket calculator and you'll find that that adds up to one pound of fat every 19 days (3,500 calories divided by 180) or 19 pounds of fat a year (365 days divided by 19). Put another way, walking just an hour a day allows me to eat about 66,000 extra calories a year without gaining an ounce!

Here's another example to show you the cumulative effect of regular exercise. Playing golf for two hours two days per week burns about 700 calories. Again, that doesn't seem like much, but over a year's time it would result in a 10-pound fat loss — provided, of course, that the food intake remained constant.

What about that, do people who exercise compensate by eating more? The answer is no, but a little explanation is required. Here's how it works, according to *Exercise Physiology*. Regular physical activity helps your brain's appetite control mechanism work better. People who exercise regularly find it easier to balance energy expenditure and food intake than sedentary people. That stands to reason, doesn't it? Active people burn more calories and, therefore, have more leeway in how much they eat. Their appestat has more time to work. On the other hand, inactive people tend to fall victim to "creeping obesity." They eat a little more than they need on a regular basis; predictably, over time, the fat piles up on their body.

Still, it's necessary to make a distinction based on the type and duration of exercise. Of course, people who perform hard physically for prolonged periods, such as lumberjacks, farm workers and endurance athletes, *do* eat more. They have to, because they often work or exercise eight hours a day, burning twice as many calories as those who are inactive. For example, marathon runners, cross-country skiers and cyclists consume about 6,000 calories a day. Nevertheless, they're among the leanest people in the world! Obviously, exercise burns the extra calories they consume *and* their extra fat stores as well.

> **The most intriguing benefit is that you continue burning extra calories even after you stop exercising.**

Importantly, however, people who train for relatively short periods don't eat more. This was shown in a study of college women whose daily calorie intake was measured during a season of competitive swimming and tennis. Swimming workouts lasted up to two hours a day; tennis practice was a little over an hour. Average daily calorie intake was monitored for each woman before and during a five-month training and competitive season. Here's what the study found: The swimmers ate about 15% more than the tennis players but, within each group, there was little change in calorie intake before and during the training and competitive season. In short, swimming and playing tennis for an hour or two didn't seem to have an appetite-stimulating effect.

Now let's move on to the more surprising — and significant — fat-loss benefits of aerobic exercise. The first — and most intriguing, perhaps — is that *you continue burning extra calories even after you stop exercising.* How many and how long is determined by the duration and intensity of the exercise.

Let's look at some examples to give you a feel for how this works. They're taken from *The Weighting Game,* an outstanding book about the finer points of weight control by medical consultant and syndicated columnist Lawrence E. Lamb, M.D. (Lyle

Stuart, 1988). You'll note they all involve aerobic exercise. That's logical, of course, because aerobic exercise is usually long and continuous. That's why it burns more calories before *and* after the activity. Aerobic exercise cranks up the metabolism and it remains elevated.

One experiment consisted of walking 10 miles at four miles per hour on a treadmill. This level of exercise increased the metabolic rate to five times the resting level. But, in addition, metabolic rate stayed an average of 15% above the basal level *for the next six hours!* You probably wouldn't want to walk 10 miles but this, again, demonstrates the fat-loss potential of walking.

More vigorous exercise will produce even greater results. A subject exercised for 80 minutes at 75% of maximum capacity. "This is a lot of exercise," Dr. Lamb observed. The after-exercise calorie loss showed it, too. Twelve hours later, the subject's energy requirement was still elevated by 19.3%!

Dr. Lamb's final example illustrates the aftereffect of mild exercise. Two men and two women exercised for 20 minutes on a stationary bicycle at 35 to 55% of their oxygen consumption maximum, which translated to 3.6 times resting energy requirement. Forty minutes after exercise, their calorie requirement remained 13% above the resting level. The subjects then pedaled for another 20 minutes. Interestingly, 40 minutes after the second exercise period, their energy requirements were more elevated, this time by 22%. In addition to showing the effect of mild physical activity, this shows the cumulative effect of several short exercise sessions. I've wondered, does my evening walk burn more calories than my noontime session?

Finally, let me tell you about the fat-loss magic I discovered reading Covert Bailey's marvelous book *Fit Or Fat?* (Houghton Mifflin, 1977). Aerobic exercise converts your body from a sugar burner to a fat burner. As noted earlier, aerobic exercise conditions your body to use more oxygen which, in turn, enables you to burn more fat. In technical terms, it increases your ability to mobilize and metabolize fatty acids. In other words, aerobic exercise enables your body to do a better job withdrawing energy from your fat deposits and burning it in your muscles.

Bailey made me aware that out-of-shape people have trouble converting fat to energy. During exercise, the untrained person burns mostly glucose or stored carbohydrate. That's part of the reason why unconditioned people are often fat. Champion endurance athletes, on the other hand, are veritable fat-burning machines. That's because, again, they are trained to utilize more oxygen. In addition, aerobic exercise stimulates the production of enzymes that convert fat to energy. Well-conditioned endurance athletes have more fat-burning enzymes and, therefore, are able to burn more stored fat.

I'm sure you've heard that marathon runners sometime "hit the wall." That means they use up the glycogen (sugar) stored in their muscles. Through training, however, distance runners can develop the capacity to use more free fatty acids for energy. In essence, aerobic exercise trains their bodies to conserve glycogen and burn fat. This ability, coupled with proper pacing in a marathon, means the athlete no longer hits the wall. It sounds like magic, I know, but it's simply another example of the body's wonderful ability to adapt to stress. In this case, the stress is endurance exercise, and the adaptations are better oxygen utilization and the development of fat-mobilizing enzymes. In short, aerobic exercise switches your body chemistry to a fat-burning mode; it alters your metabolism in a way that naturally produces a leaner body.

Now you see why I give equal billing to aerobics and weights in my training program, although it wasn't always this way. As you already know, my conversion was a long time coming. Hopefully, I've shortened yours.

Now let's move on to the equally important — but often misunderstood — role of weight training in the quest to achieve permanent leanness.

THE ROLE OF WEIGHTS

As already mentioned, Covert Bailey's book *Fit Or Fat?* influenced my training greatly. Nevertheless, I found the book puzzling in one important respect: Covert Bailey's approach to fat control did not include weight training.

This puzzled me because Bailey was quite aware of the role of muscle in the fat-loss process. "Of all the calories burned in the body," he wrote, "90% are burned by muscle, even if you are sedentary." What's more, he emphasized that muscle tissue burns calories even when you sleep. "Clearly, if you want to get rid of calories," he summarized, "you should look to the *quantity* and quality of your muscle." (Emphasis mine.) And still, he didn't recommend weight training.

Lifting weights, Bailey counseled, is for strength and bulk. For weight control and fitness his prescription was short and simple: aerobic endurance exercise. You've heard of good cholesterol and bad cholesterol. Well, Bailey characterized weight training as the bad form of exercise, anaerobic exercise, which he described, correctly, as short-term exercise which burns few calories and almost no fat. He also lumped weight training in with spot reducing.

"The end result is a *larger* muscle with the same fat deposit sitting on top of it," he said.

Spot reducing, of course, doesn't work. The theory of spot reducing is that localized exercise reduces the fat stored in the area of the exercise. Unfortunately, according to *Exercise Physiology,* the textbook cited earlier, "There is simply no evidence that fatty acids are released to a greater degree from the fat pads directly over the exercising muscles."

The fallacy of spot reducing has been demonstrated by comparing the circumference and subcutaneous fat stores on the right and left forearms of high-caliber tennis players. As almost everyone would expect, the playing arm was found to contain more muscle. Spot reducing advocates, however, would be surprised to learn that fatfold thickness was the same on both arms.

In another experiment described in *Exercise Physiology,* fat biopsies were taken from the abdominal region, upper back and buttocks in subjects who performed sit-ups every day for 27 days. Again, the fat cells in the exercised abdominal region did not become smaller than those in the unexercised buttocks and upper back regions.

Covert Bailey explained why spot reducing doesn't work: "The subcutaneous fat lying on top of a muscle doesn't 'belong' to that particular muscle. It belongs to the entire body." In other words, fat is systemic, it's deposited all over your body; and the only way to reduce the size of the fat cells in one area is to reduce them all over your body. Covert Bailey had this exactly right. Still, that doesn't mean there's no role for weight training in the fat-loss process.

Weight training builds and maintains your muscle tissue, thereby keeping your calorie-burn level up high.

Actually, Covert Bailey had all the facts right. He knew that muscle makes you lean. He knew that the more muscle you have the more calories you burn, because muscle cells are active cells. They maintain a slight continuous contraction (muscle tone) even while at rest or during sleep. They burn calories 24 hours a day. Fat cells, on the other hand, are inactive. They serve mainly as a storage space for more fat. And they burn very few calories.

Here's an excerpt from my book *Ripped 2* to show how muscle makes you lean. "A person with three percent body fat burns more calories per pound of body weight than a person with 25 percent body fat. So a meal that would make the person with 25 percent fat fatter may actually make the person with three percent fat, and more calorie-burning muscle tissue, leaner. In effect, the person with three percent fat speeds along on a high-powered racing engine, burning fuel like mad, while the person with 25 percent fat plods along on an under-powered economy engine."

Again, Covert Bailey had all the facts, but for some reason he wasn't able to put two and two together to get four. He didn't take the next step and ask the question: What's the best way to build muscle? The answer, of course, is weight training.

As Dr. Lamb wrote in *The Weighting Game*: "It goes back to the ancient story of the young man who grew strong by lifting a small bull calf each day. As the bull grew, so did the young man, until by the time the bull was full grown, the young man's body was bulging with muscles." That quaint story, of course, embodies the basis for all weight training. A muscle grows as it is forced to work against progressive resistance. That's the "overload principle." A muscle adjusts, grows, as it is forced to work against increasing resistance. The result is bigger and stronger muscles — and more calorie-burning capacity.

A few years after reading *Fit Or Fat?* I attended a seminar Covert Bailey presented to a group of dentists. Apparently, he still hadn't gotten the message at that time, because he was still poking fun at weight trainers. At the end of the presentation, I gave him an autographed copy of *Ripped* in which I had described my reduction to 2.4% body fat through a program of diet and weight training — and almost no aerobic exercise. I never met Covert Bailey again, and I don't know whether he read my book. He did, however, subsequently change his view on weight training. Bailey's latest book, written with Lea Bishop, *The Fit Or Fat Woman* (Houghton Mifflin, 1989), recommends a three-pronged approach to fat control: aerobic exercise, balanced dieting and, yes, "weight lifting/bodybuilding to increase fat-burning muscle and shape body contours."

In *Fit Or Fat Woman*, Bailey and Bishop tell it like it is. As Covert did earlier, they argue forcefully for aerobic exercise: "Anyone who omits aerobic exercise from a fat-control program will fail in the long run."

This time, however, they acknowledge that there's a problem: "Aerobic exercise... stimulates only a slight increase in muscle." They now recommend weight training to solve that problem. Weight training is important, they say, because it builds and maintains muscle. In their words: "The changes in muscle [brought about by weight training] do have a long-term effect on body chemistry by: [among other things] increasing the amount of muscle so that the body uses more calories."

The muscle maintenance effect of strength training is especially important when you're dieting. It's equally important as you get older and the muscles have a natural tendency to atrophy.

In *The Weighting Game,* Dr. Lamb warns dieters: "It is inevitable that if you are inactive, and simply reduce your caloric intake to establish a negative calorie balance, you will lose body protein." In short, if you try to lose fat by diet alone, you'll lose muscle, too.

To demonstrate this, Dr. Lamb cites a study which involved 25 overweight women. Their lean body mass was determined with calipers and underwater weighing. The women were then divided into three groups, and each group was placed on a different weight-loss program: diet only, exercise only and a combination of diet and exercise. The diet group had their caloric intake set 500 calories below maintenance level. The exercise group didn't diet, but increased their exercise enough to burn 500 additional calories. The combination group cut their dietary intake 250 calories and increased their exercise level sufficiently to burn 250 additional calories. So all three groups had a negative balance of 500. Here's what happened after 16 weeks.

All three groups lost about the same amount of weight: The diet-only group lost an average of 11.7 pounds, the exercise group 10.6 pounds, and the combination group 12 pounds. The important point, however, is what happened to their lean body weight. The diet-only group lost 2.42 pounds of lean body weight. The combination group *gained* one pound of lean tissue. And the exercise group gained two pounds of lean body mass. This means, of course, that the diet group lost only 9 pounds of fat (11.7 less 2.42) while the exercise and combination groups lost about 13 pounds of fat.

"The point to learn from this study," says Dr. Lamb, "is that if you really need to lose pounds of fat, you should combine exercise with your diet program." He explains that diet alone causes loss of metabolically-active muscle tissue, but that the loss can be prevented with exercise. It's the old story: Use it or lose it.

Dr. Lamb also points out that this positive result in the study cited came about even though the exercise involved was low in intensity. He adds that the kind of exercise is important. "It should [use] all of your muscle, to insure that some muscles don't enlarge at the expense of muscles that are losing protein."

Bodybuilding, of course, systematically trains all of the body's muscles. When you walk, jog or bike, your leg muscles do most of the work. Your upper body just goes along for the ride, so to speak. Bodybuilding, however, done properly, works your forearms, your calves and everything in between.

Dr. Lamb doesn't beat around the bush; he says that weight training *should* be a part of your fat-loss program. Endurance exercise is important, but it's not the answer to total body fitness, nor is it the only exercise necessary to help maintain a balance be-

Weight training,
done properly,
works your
forearms...

your calves...

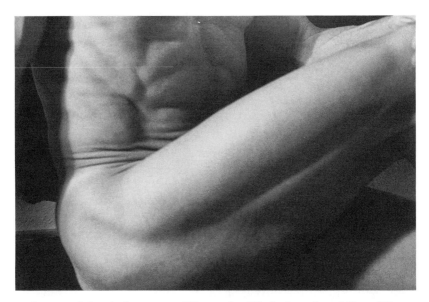

and everything in between. *Photos by Chris Lund and Carol Bass.*

tween calorie intake and outgo. Dr. Lamb explains it this way: "Endurance exercises have their greatest effect in helping you eliminate calories by driving your catabolic system. Strength exercises help you through their anabolic action in muscle building, which, in turn, increases your near-basal calorie requirements."

Catabolism is defined as "destructive metabolism" and anabolism is "constructive metabolism." So that's a doctor's way of saying that strength training complements the fat-burning action of aerobic exercise by building calorie-burning muscle tissue. Weight training builds and maintains your muscle tissue, thereby keeping your calorie-burn level turned up high.

This is especially important as you age, according to Dr. Lamb. It's common sense. Weight training slows the tendency we all have to lose muscle with age. With less muscle, our bodies burn fewer calories. So if we continue eating the same amount as we get older, we fall victim to middle-aged spread. That is, unless we preserve our calorie-burning muscle tissue through weight training.

In his book, Dr. Lamb offers the example of Magnus Levy, the British physiologist who (in 1906) defined basal metabolism, as a precisely documented example of muscle loss with age and its effect on calorie requirements. Levy carefully measured and recorded his resting calorie requirement at age 26 and again at 76.

At 26, he weighed 148.5 pounds and burned 1,608 calories each day when at rest. At 76, he weighed 132 pounds and burned only

1,248 calories. In other words, over the course of 50 years he lost 16.5 pounds and 360 units of calorie-burning capacity (1,608 calories less 1,248).

Dr. Lamb says exercise physiologists can calculate the change in Levy's fat-free body weight on the basis of his basal calorie requirements at 26 and 76. I won't burden you with the formula, but the answer is that his lean body weight dropped from 115 pounds at 26 to 89.4 pounds at 76. His body fat was 22% at age 26 and 32% at age 76. Lamb says that is a normal change for a person who doesn't follow a strength training program.

Now consider the practical effect of Levy's loss of muscle and calorie-burning capacity. As noted, his daily resting energy requirement dropped by 360 calories. That means if he wanted to keep from gaining body fat, he had two choices. He could increase his daily activity level by 360 calories — walking six miles a day would probably do it — or he could eat 360 fewer calories.

That's the choice most people face as they age. There is, of course, another alternative. Says Dr. Lamb, "You can avoid this problem by including strength exercise in your program to maintain your muscle size as you go through life. These are not endurance exercises, such as walking, but exercises that cause your muscles to work against resistance." He means, of course, weight training.

This goes back to what we said earlier: Use it or lose it. As I explained in *Ripped 2,* muscle fibers work on the all-or-none principle. A muscle is either completely "on" or completely "off." There is no such thing as a half-hearted or halfway contraction. Muscle fibers work as hard as possible — or not at all.

The body uses its muscle fibers sparingly. It always enlists the minimum number necessary for the task at hand. The rest of the fibers don't contract; they remain off. That's why Dr. Lamb advises, "You do need to keep stimulating the muscles at the maximum level of their capacity." Because, again, you'll lose the muscle fibers you don't use.

Your muscles adjust — grow larger or smaller — to meet the requirements asked of them. "If that is just lifting a martini," Dr. Lamb cautions, "you'll soon be back to martini muscles again." And, chances are, you'll develop a beer belly to match.

Obviously, if you wanted martini muscles and a beer belly, you wouldn't be reading this. So let's get to the specifics of the Lean-For-Life diet and exercise program.

CHAPTER IV
THE EATING PLAN

Photo by Chris Lund.

CHAPTER IV:
THE EATING PLAN

THE EATING PLAN

Once you grasp the idea, eating for leanness and health is really quite simple — and enjoyable as well. Unfortunately, for one reason or another, many people haven't learned — or just don't practice — a few basic principles. You can see this at your local supermarket. Look at the contents of the shopping carts in the check-out lines.

In *Ripped 3,* I observed that your body tends to mirror your life-style. Well, in a similar fashion, the body behind the shopping cart usually reflects the food inside. Think about this on your next trip to the supermarket. Look at the contents of the carts around you without looking at the person, or the reverse: look at the person first. If the cart is full of soda pop, potato chips, ice cream, fatty meats and various and sundry refined and packaged products, it's a good bet that the person pushing it is overweight. On the other hand, if the body behind the cart is lean and healthy-looking, the odds are that the cart is loaded with fruit, vegetables and whole-grain products, along with skimmed milk and maybe a little fish, chicken or extra-lean beef. Plus, you're not likely to find many boxed or packaged foods.

Once you know the kind of food a person eats, you can pretty well predict whether that person will be lean or fat.

The body/shopping-cart relationship usually holds true, because what really counts is the type of food one eats. Once you know the kind of food a person eats, you can pretty well predict whether that person will be lean or fat. Believe it or not, you don't need to know how much the person eats. The type of food eaten is the key. The amount is much less important. That's because if you eat the right things, you can almost eat as much as you want and still lose weight; it's actually hard to overeat. What happens is you become full and satisfied before you take in more calories than you burn.

Through the example given above, I've indirectly described the eating style that keeps me lean and will do the same for you. In essence, my approach is to eat whole foods the way they are grown

— nothing removed or added. That's because most foods in their natural form are not fattening. For the most part, it's only when alterations are made that food becomes fattening.

Wild animals are rarely fat (have you noticed?). One reason is because they eat foods in their natural state, with nothing removed or added. It's only when they are domesticated, and fed processed and refined foods, that they tend to get fat.

Can you think of a food in its natural form that is high in calories? Avocados, nuts, seeds and whole milk are a few, but there aren't many. It's usually when food is altered that it becomes fattening. Typically, that means removing the fiber and adding fat and sweeteners.

Okay, you say, but what is it exactly that makes whole foods non-fattening? First, they are usually low in fat. As you probably know, fat is fattening. Next, carbohydrates in whole foods are "natural," just the way they come from the earth. Unlike refined and processed foods, they are "packaged" with dietary fiber; all the "roughage" and "bulk" is still present. Carbohydrate and fiber, as we'll soon see, are your powerful allies in the battle of the bulge.

I should tell you from the outset that the Lean-For-Life diet has a strong vegetarian emphasis, yet it's a very enjoyable diet. Most of the food comes from plants, but some animal products are consumed as well. For example, non-fat dairy products are included for texture and nutritional balance, and lean meat and fish are used, in small amounts, for flavoring. What's more, a little salt from time to time is fine for most people. As I said earlier, this is an enjoyable diet. I don't eat food unless it tastes good, and I wouldn't ask you to either.

So, in summary, the eating plan can be described as low fat, natural carbohydrate and near vegetarian. Now let's get to the details. We'll examine the various elements of the eating plan and see why they help you get lean and stay that way.

Why does eating fat make you fat?

The main reason is that fat contains more calories per gram than any other kind of food. Each gram of fat contains nine calories, while one gram of protein or carbohydrate contains only four calories. Fat is a calorie-dense food. It provides a large number of calories in a small volume. Simply put, if you eat carbohydrates or protein, especially in whole foods, you can eat more than twice as much — without increasing the number of calories.

For example, it's not carbohydrate foods such as bread and potatoes that make you fat, it's the butter you add. It's not the salad that's fattening, it's the oily dressing on top. Whole milk is an excellent source of protein, but it's also fattening. That's because it contains 3.5% fat which, difficult as it may be to believe, accounts for almost 50% of the calories. (Remember that most of the weight in milk is water.) If you eliminate most of the fat by consuming skimmed milk, you'll get all the protein, but 40% fewer calories.

To make matters even worse, fat stimulates your appetite; it encourages you to overeat because it tastes so good. Ask yourself, would you be inclined to eat more baked potato with sour cream or without?

And there's more. Recent research shows that fat calories are more easily converted to body fat than other calories. Studies at Harvard and Stanford Medical Schools found that excess body weight is more closely linked to fat consumption than to calorie consumption.

Tufts University Diet & Nutrition Letter summed up the two studies like this: "What it comes down to is that if two men require 2,000 calories a day each, the one who eats a greater proportion of his 2,000 calories as fat is more likely to end up with body fat than the one who takes in more of his calories as carbohydrate." Why is this? What's the explanation?

Experiments at the University of Massachusetts Medical School show that dietary fat can be turned into body fat so easily the process only uses up 3% of the calories consumed, while it takes 23% of calories consumed to turn carbohydrate into fat stores. In other words, if you consume 100 excess carbohydrate calories, only 77 of them will end up as body fat; but if you consume the same number of calories as fat, 97 will turn up on your body as fat. That's a difference of 25% and, over time, it can add up to many extra pounds of body fat.

In his book *Fit-or-Fat Target Diet* (Houghton Mifflin, 1984), Covert Bailey calls fat "the dieter's number one enemy." You can see why. Yes, indeed — and not surprising — fat is fattening!

What are the fat-loss benefits of natural carbohydrates?

First, we've already seen that carbohydrates, any kind, are less fattening than fat — one gram of carbohydrate has less than half the calories of a gram of fat. Plus, carbohydrates are harder for the body to convert to fat; when you eat carbohydrates, fewer calories turn up on your body as fat. Obviously, if a dieter is faced with the choice of sugar or butter, both fattening foods, the lesser of the two evils would be sugar, which is pure carbohydrate. Butter, of course, is almost all fat.

We've all heard statements along this line: "I need to go on a diet and lose some weight; I think I'll start by cutting down on carbohydrates." That's the wrong approach, of course. The truth is that carbohydrates can help you lose weight. In *Ripped 2,* I included a study conducted at Michigan State University by Dr. Olaf Mickelsen, a professor of nutrition. I'm going to repeat it here, because it's such a wonderful demonstration that carbohydrates are, in fact, a dieter's best friend.

Here's Professor Mickelsen's report: "Contrary to what most people think, bread in large amounts is an ideal food in a weight-reducing regimen. Recent work in our laboratory indicates that slightly overweight young men lost weight in a painless and practically effortless manner when they included 12 slices of bread per day in their program. The bread was eaten with their meals. As a result, they became satisfied before they consumed their usual quota of calories. The subjects were admonished to restrict those foods that were concentrated sources of energy [that is, very high in calories]; otherwise, they were free to eat as much as they desired."

Dr. Mickelsen's eight-week study involved 16 young men. Eight were given a high-fiber bread; they lost an average of 19.4 pounds. The other eight were served a low-fiber bread; their average weight loss was 13.7 pounds.

There's something more at work in the Michigan State study than simply the number of calories per gram of carbohydrate, or how hard the body has to work to convert carbohydrates to fat. Jane Brody, in her *Nutrition Book* (W.W. Norton, 1981), puts her finger on it: "Carbohydrate foods — at least the starches, fruits, and vegetables — fill both your physical and psychological need for food. They make you feel like you've eaten something. They fill your stomach, stick to your ribs, give you something to chew on." In short, bread filled the stomachs of the college students, but it did something even more important: It satisfied their psychological needs as well. That's the beauty of carbohydrates; they make you feel satisfied, without giving you too many calories.

You noticed, I'm sure, that the students eating the high-fiber bread lost about 40% more weight than those eating the low-fiber bread. Remember what I said earlier about the carbohydrate/fiber combination? Dr. Mickelsen's study demonstrates the effectiveness of this combination as a fat fighter.

Fiber is the non-digestible part of plants. It contains almost no calories. Fiber passes through the digestive tract into the large intestine virtually unchanged. When it reaches the large intestine, only a minimal number of calories are absorbed through the intestinal wall. Fiber is found in all whole grains, legumes, fruits and vegetables. It goes without saying, therefore, that foods high in fiber tend to be low in calories.

In addition to being low in calories, high-fiber foods are bulky and absorb water as they pass through the digestive tract. That's important, because calorie-free water and fiber provide the bulk that fills you up before you get more calories than you need. Obviously, that explains why the students eating the high-fiber bread lost more weight. The fiber, and the water it absorbed, left less room in their stomachs for calorie-containing foods.

In refined and processed foods, much of the fiber is removed. As the Michigan State study showed, this is counter-productive from a weight loss standpoint. When fiber is removed from food, calorie content increases in relation to the volume. That, of course, makes it easier to consume more calories. Before you know it, you have overshot your caloric needs.

The apple study is additional proof that the more we refine foods—the more fattening food becomes.

Now let me tell you about another study which further explains what happens when we alter foods by removing the fiber and bulk, thereby increasing the caloric density. This study involves apples and was performed at the Royal Infirmary in Bristol, England.

The following description of the study appeared in *Jane Brody's Nutrition Book*: "Ten healthy people were given test 'meals' of either whole apples, puréed apples (applesauce) or apple juice. Each meal contained the same amount of sugar. It took 17 minutes to eat the apples, six minutes to down the purée and 1½ minutes to drink the juice. It should come as no surprise to learn that the individuals reported greater satisfaction after eating the apples than after drinking the juice, with the purée providing an intermediate level of satiety."

Importantly, this experiment went beyond the subjective feelings of the test subjects. The researchers actually recorded changes in blood sugar and insulin levels to determine if there was a physiological basis for the different degrees of hunger satisfaction.

"Blood sugar rose to similar levels after all three meals," Jane Brody reported, "but the insulin level of the blood rose twice as high after the juice than after the whole apple. One to three hours later, the blood sugar levels dropped — back to normal after the apples, but to a level distinctly below normal after the juice. An intermediate but below-normal blood sugar level occurred after the purée."

Commenting on the significance of the different blood sugar and insulin levels in the three groups, Brody wrote: "These below-normal levels [of blood sugar], called rebound hypoglycemia, are usually associated with feelings of hunger. Thus, the fiber in the whole apples reduced the demand for insulin and produced a longer lasting feeling of satiety." In other words, whole apples produced long-term hunger satisfaction. In contrast, apple juice and apple sauce, both refined carbohydrates, caused low blood sugar and only short-term satisfaction; soon after eating refined carbohydrates you're hungry again.

The apple study, of course, is additional proof that the more we refine food (moving further away from the natural form in which it comes from the garden, orchard or field), the more fattening food becomes. Here are some more examples to illustrate this point:

A cup of raw grapes (153 grams) directly from the vine provides 106 calories. But remove the water from the grapes and consume one cup (165 grams) of raisins, and you get four times as many calories, 477 versus 106. Now add sugar, lard and flour — all refined foods with the water and bulk removed — to make raisin pie, and you're really talking serious calories.

The same thing happens as you move from whole grains to white bread to cake. The calories increase with each refining step as more bulk is removed and sweeteners added.

Moreover, as mentioned in connection with fat, refined carbohydrates, such as sugar, stimulate the appetite and encourage overeating. (The same holds true for honey.) The more carbohydrates are refined, the more likely you are to eat large quantities without being aware of it. For example, as the apple study showed, you're likely to consume more calories drinking apple juice, a refined product, than if you eat the whole apple. You're tempted to drink more apple juice, of course, because it's sweeter. Plus, no chewing is required, the juice goes down fast, and it takes up less room in your stomach.

Sybil Ferguson, founder of The Diet Centers, perhaps summarizes the message best. She recommends eating carbohydrates in "Mother Nature's wrapper." All I can add to that is — amen!

Why near vegetarian?

The reason is simple. Basically it's this: Animal foods — meat, dairy products and eggs — usually contain substantial quantities of fat, and no fiber. They are concentrated-calorie foods. They pack a lot of calories in a small volume. That, of course, makes it easy to overeat. On the other hand, vegetarian or plant foods are generally low in fat and high in fiber. As we've seen, that combination keeps you lean. Let's look at some meat-based and vegetarian meals to see how they stack up.

First, compare a plate full of rice and beans (one cup brown rice and one-half cup beans) with three ounces of T-bone steak. The calories are about the same. Both contain a little more than 300. The similarity stops there, however. The rice and beans combination contains about two grams of fiber; since fiber is found only in plant foods, the T-bone steak, of course, contains none. And here's the real kicker: The rice and beans contain less than two grams of fat; there's 31.5 grams in the T-bone steak! The fat content explains why the volume is so much greater in the rice and beans. A plate full of rice and beans fills your stomach. Three ounces of T-bone steak leaves you wanting more.

Here's another eye-opening comparison. A typical American meat-and-potato meal contains about 1,500 calories: six ounces of steak, a potato with butter, one-half cup carrots, salad with blue cheese dressing and apple pie. Let's compare this with the following vegetarian meal: one cup of brown rice and lentils, two slices of whole-grain bread with margarine, one-half cup of carrots and peas, a lettuce and tomato salad with dressing, a fruit salad containing one banana, one apple, one orange, two tablespoons of raisins and a half-dozen walnuts. The latter meal contains only 890 calories. Wow! That's 610 less than the steak dinner and, of course, you'd be positively stuffed after eating such a vegetarian meal. This comparison illustrates the huge amount of food a vegetarian can consume without exceeding the body's caloric needs.

But be careful. That doesn't mean all vegetarian meals are low calorie. The fat-is-fattening rule still applies. If you gorge on nuts and seeds — one cup raw almonds contains 77 grams of fat and 849 calories; a like amount of dried sunflower seeds has 69 grams fat and 812 calories — you will get fat!

And fiber still counts. For example, vegetable oil labels trumpet: "No Cholesterol." They don't mention that oil is also fiber free. Actually, it's pure fat. Consume one tablespoon of corn oil and you get 126 calories. By comparison, you could eat a whole cup of the corn itself, with all the fiber and bulk intact, and get approximately the same number of calories. So, you see, eating vegetarian foods doesn't guarantee leanness *if the foods are processed or naturally contain a lot of fat.* You still have to eat smart. Otherwise, you can end up a fat vegetarian.

In *Ripped 2,* I observed that I feel better when I don't eat meat. For one thing, my bowels function better. Because of its fat content and lack of fiber, meat slows the elimination process. Plus, there's good evidence that man wasn't made to eat meat.

Dr. Dean Ornish, in his book *Reversing Heart Disease* (Random House, 1990), points out that many anthropologists believe our ancestors were primarily vegetarians. For example, our teeth are more like those of plant eaters than flesh eaters. They're better designed for grinding than for cutting. Plus, carnivores have a short, smooth digestive tract so they can digest meat and get rid of the waste products fast. Our intestines are long and convoluted, which allows us to digest high-fiber plant foods that take a long time to be broken down and absorbed. The problem is that meat decomposes rapidly and our digestive tract keeps the toxic waste products in the body far longer than is the case with carnivores.

What's more, according to Dr. Ornish, a low-fat vegetarian diet is the world's healthiest diet for most adults. In addition to keeping you lean, he says, there is a considerable body of scientific evidence that a low-fat vegetarian diet reduces the risk of heart disease, high blood pressure, diabetes, colon cancer and other ailments. If you'd like more details, I highly recommend that you read Dr. Ornish's book.

But what about protein?

In my early years in weight training I consumed so much protein powder that the local health food store gave me a discount. I remember attending the *Strength & Health* picnic that Bob Hoffman hosted each year at Brookside Park, near his home in Dover, Penn. Bob Hoffman, you'll remember, was the editor and publisher of *Strength & Health* magazine and a pioneer in the food supplement business. One of the attractions at his annual picnic was free protein drink. Made with milk, ice cream and Hoffman's Hi-Proteen powder (chocolate flavor), it was delicious!

Bob Maher, a New Mexico weightlifting buddy who attended the picnic with me, suggested, "Let's make a meal of this; we won't have to buy dinner." It didn't take much to convince me. As I recall we filled up on Hoffman's Hi-Proteen mixture... and had dinner, too. We were convinced, you see, that extra protein would make our muscles grow faster. The ice cream, of course, was an added incentive, but by no means essential. At that stage my friend and I would have eaten or drunk just about anything — if we thought it would make us bigger and stronger. Yes, those were fun times. I wouldn't trade them for the world. Nevertheless, Bob and I did have a few things to learn about protein.

Protein, from the Greek word meaning "of prime importance," is essential for body repair and maintenance. All of us, athletes and couch potatoes alike, need protein. Protein is formed from building blocks called amino acids. There are approximately 20 different kinds of amino acids. Your body can make 12 of these amino acids. That's why the other eight are called "essential amino acids" — the body cannot manufacture them, so they must be provided by our diet. What my friend, Bob, and I didn't know, however, is that most people eat at least twice as much protein as they need. Most bodybuilders probably consume more than three

This photo of me lifting almost 300 pounds overhead was taken around the time Bob Maher and I attended the *Strength & Health* picnic.

times the amount of protein that their bodies require.

Found in the cells of all animals and plants, proteins containing all the essential amino acids are called complete proteins; the others are called incomplete proteins. Animal proteins such as those found in eggs, milk and meat are examples of complete proteins. The proteins in plant foods are incomplete; they lack some essential amino acids. That's not a problem for vegetarians, however. All the essential amino acids can be obtained by consuming a variety of plant foods.

Of the essential amino acids, only three — lysine, tryptophan and methionine — are critical, since the others are plentiful in most foods. The amino acids in plant foods are just as good as those in animal foods. The problem, as mentioned, is that no one plant food contains all the critical amino acids. You have to eat a variety of plant foods to obtain all the necessary amino acids. But, again, that's no problem.

All you have to do is remember that beans, any kind, are high in lysine, but low in tryptophan and methionine. Grains (bread, rice, pasta, etc.) are low in lysine, but high in tryptophan and methionine. A meal of rice and beans, therefore, provides complete protein, no different from the protein found in eggs or meat.

How do you ensure you're getting enough protein? "It's easy," says Dr. Dean Ornish, "just eat any grains and any legumes (you want) sometime during the day.... As long as you consume enough non-sugar calories to maintain your ideal body weight, then you will likely be eating enough protein."

Actually, the formula I now use is even simpler. I have a little skimmed milk, non-fat yogurt or a few ounces of extra lean beef, fish or chicken with each meal. The essential amino acids in these animal foods complement the amino acids in the plant foods that make up the bulk of my diet. The combination gives me all the complete protein I need.

That's all there is to it! As long as you don't starve yourself — you already know I don't recommend that — protein intake is no problem on a balanced diet of vegetarian foods, especially if small amounts of low-fat animal foods are added. (Infants, growing children, pregnant women and nursing mothers are special cases. They do need more than the usual amount of protein. Burn patients and people who have had surgery may also have higher protein requirements.)

So, again, don't worry about protein. A balanced diet of vegetarian foods combined with small portions of skimmed milk or lean meat will supply all your dietary needs, including protein. That was corroborated recently by the recommendation of the

Eat a low-fat, vegetarian-oriented diet and you'll not only be well nourished, you'll be able to eat all you want without getting fat. *Photo by Allen Hughes.*

Physicians Committee for Responsible Medicine, a Washington-based group of 3,000 doctors promoting preventive medicine.

Remember the Basic Four Food Groups (fruits and vegetables, bread, milk and meat) used by nutritionists to show you how to eat right? Well, this physicians' committee is urging the U.S. Department of Agriculture to revamp the groupings to concentrate on fruit, vegetables, legumes and whole grains, and make meat and dairy products optional. "[The traditional food groups] tend to sustain something we ought not to be doing — eating a diet high in animal fat and protein and lacking in fiber," said T. Colin Campbell, a professor of nutritional biochemistry at Cornell University. Professor Campbell and the doctors' group cite mounting evidence that diets high in fat and low in fiber increase the risk of heart disease, cancer, diabetes and obesity.

The physicians' committee confirms that nutritional requirements, including protein, can be met on a plant-based diet. The average American, they say, eats twice as much protein as needed. They propose four new food groups: grains, vegetables, legumes and fruits. And listen to this: "A unique feature of this new guide," the committee report said, "is that it does not rely on any admonition to use particular foods in moderation, since all the foods in the guide... can be consumed with impunity."

Does that sound familiar? In other words, eat a low-fat, vegetarian-oriented diet and you'll not only be well nourished, you'll be able to eat all you want without getting fat.

(If you'd like more information on protein requirements, *Ripped 2* contains a complete discussion of muscle-building nutrition.)

What about taste and eating pleasure?

Eating enjoyment is important — very important! You simply won't stick with a diet you don't like. As the name implies, the Lean-For-Life eating plan is for the long haul... forever! It's not a diet you follow for a few months, and then go back to eating fattening foods.

There's more than a little truth in the old saying, "The way to a man's heart is through his stomach." Food satisfies more than the physical appetite. All of us — men and women — feel better, more contented, when we're full and satisfied.

There's absolutely no need to eat food that doesn't taste good.

Some claim they eat to live, but I don't believe it's true for very many people. My guess is that most people are like me: they live to eat. Eating is one of life's great pleasures. It's built into our system. We're programmed to enjoy food.

A boring, tasteless diet, therefore, really makes no sense. It just won't work. It's psychologically unsound. I wouldn't attempt to follow such a diet, and I don't recommend it to others. Eating the Lean-For-Life way is a pleasure. That's one of the reasons why it works so well. I enjoy every meal, and it's important that you do the same. There's absolutely no need to eat food that doesn't taste good.

I've already explained why this eating plan will make you lean while satisfying your nutritional needs. Now let's look at why it's psychologically satisfying as well.

Whole grains, fruits and vegetables, which make up the major part of my diet, fill you up without giving you too many calories. The fiber and bulk in these foods guarantee that you never leave the table physically hungry. Your stomach is full. That's not true of the eat-a-little-bit-less-of-everything diet that some recommend. On a mostly vegetarian diet, you don't have to rely on willpower and self-control. You won't want more; you'll be pleasantly full, even stuffed.

Chewing is another advantage that bulky, fiber-filled foods have over refined foods. Chewing adds eating satisfaction. We need to chew.

Remember the study involving apples, apple sauce and apple juice? One reason why the subjects reported greater satisfaction after eating the apples was that, unlike apple juice and to a lesser degree apple sauce, you have to chew an apple. Chewing gives you time to savor the delicious, sweet flavor. Refined apple juice and apple sauce, on the other hand, are gone before you know it, and before you're really satisfied.

The situation with almost all processed and refined food is the same: little chewing is required. Basically, you just put it in your mouth and swallow. That makes it hard to satisfy yourself psychologically without exceeding your caloric needs.

The bread study performed at Michigan State is another case in point. The bulky, high-fiber bread made the students feel more satisfied than the refined, low-fiber variety. They were satisfied with less food when they ate the high-fiber bread because it gave them more to chew on. That's an advantage that most of the foods in the Lean-For-Life diet have in common. Chewing satisfaction, therefore, is another plus for this diet.

Americans are used to strong tastes. Sugar, salt and fat, all powerful appetite stimulants, permeate the typical American diet. When you get near a fast-food restaurant, the smell is in the air. You don't have to walk inside the restaurant. The aroma almost carries you in. (That's the idea, of course.)

At my office, when the wind is right, I can smell the fast-food restaurant two blocks away. And I'll have to admit, I'm tempted.

You would be, too.

Actually, that's another plus for low-fat vegetarian foods. Whole grains, fruits and vegetables have a mild, subtle, yet pleasant taste. Plant foods give your appetite control mechanism a chance to work. Your body tells you when you've had enough. With highly seasoned and refined foods, on the other hand, you're almost forced to overeat. You're overpowered.

Nevertheless, like most people, I crave the stronger flavors I grew up with. So I compromise, but in a way that gives me the best of both worlds.

I use flavor enhancers. They add taste, but few extra calories. I'll give you a few examples here, and some more in the menu plans at the end of the book.

As I said earlier, my diet is mostly, but not entirely, vegetarian. You don't have to be a total vegetarian to derive the major benefits of a vegetarian diet. It does no harm to add a little meat, fish or chicken to a vegetable-based meal to give added flavor. That's a switch for most Americans. They use meat as the main course, whereas I use animal food to add flavor only. And it doesn't take much. For example, an ounce or two of extra lean beef adds a great deal of eating pleasure to grains, beans or vegetables. The trick is this: keep in mind that the plant-based food, not the meat, is the main course.

In the same way, I use the "meatless" meat, chicken and fish products now available in most health food stores and many supermarket chains. These are purely vegetarian foods made to look and taste like sausages, burgers, bacon, chicken, fish, etc. Some of these meat analogues are made with soybeans, a high-protein legume used extensively in Asia; others are a combination of grains, low-fat dairy products and egg whites. They're surprisingly good. If you didn't know better, you'd think you were eating the real thing.

That's the problem. Most of them are too much like the real thing. They're high in fat and loaded with salt! So I use them the same way I do meat: as flavor enhancers only, and not as the main course.

For example, I sometimes buy a meatless chicken product. It's formed like mini-drumsticks. According to the package, five pieces make up one serving. Unfortunately, that's 230 calories with 13 grams of fat and 640 milligrams of sodium. The solution is simple, however. I just break up two pieces, 40% of the serving size, and mix them in with vegetables or a grain dish. That provides all the flavor I want, but less than 100 extra calories. It's a great compromise. Again, it gives me the best of both worlds.

A lot of flavor in these vegetarian meat products, of course, comes from the high sodium content. According to Dr. Dean Ornish, salt is not as big a health problem as many people think. He says that less than one-fourth of the people who have high blood pressure are "salt sensitive." That means if you don't have high blood pressure, there's probably no need for you to limit your salt intake drastically.

Most processed and refined foods, as you probably know, are loaded with salt. However, natural foods (the way they come in nature) are low in sodium, so for most people it does no harm to add a little salt. I never use the salt shaker, but I do like salsa on my grains and vegetables. I always check the label, however, to make sure I'm not adding sugar or oil. The brand I use is made with tomatoes, green chile, onions, jalapeño peppers, salt, vinegar and garlic. That's it. For a few extra milligrams of sodium — and almost no additional calories — salsa adds a lot of eating enjoyment. It's another good compromise, one that keeps me satisfied — and lean.

The introduction to one of the cookbooks in my wife's library says, "You, in fact, are the most important ingredient in any recipe." That's a good thought to bear in mind. It's one thing for me to tell you how I satisfy my taste buds. In the final analysis, however, it's up to you to create meals to your liking. That should be no problem, though. Just try the suggestions given here and those that follow.

You don't have to count calories because your body does the counting for you.

Master the theory behind the eating plan. Then use your imagination. Experiment. Make changes. Soon you'll be creating delicious and satisfying Lean-For-Life meals all your own.

Do I have to count calories?

No, you don't. As we've already seen, the important thing to focus on is the *type* of food in your diet. Eat mainly low-fat, natural carbohydrate, vegetarian foods and you'll rarely exceed your caloric needs. You'll actually find it hard to overeat. You don't have to count calories, because your body — the size of your stomach and your natural appetite control mechanism — does the counting for you. I have, however, found some auxiliary techniques that make my natural calorie-control mechanism function better — primarily by giving it time to work. They're just common sense, but I believe you'll find them helpful.

I plan each meal and only put on the table the food I intend to eat. This practice has saved me thousands of extra calories over the years. If I had to list only one calorie-coping trick, the one that has helped me the most, this would be it. I'm almost always satisfied when I finish a meal. If extra food is sitting in front of me, however, I'll probably eat it, too — even though I don't *really* want more food. Leaving serving dishes on the table, boardinghouse style, is an invitation to overeat. As I wrote in *Ripped 2*: "If you're not careful, you'll be like my favorite comic strip character, Hagar. He got up too much momentum [at breakfast] and slid on into lunch."

Putting the tempting extras away beforehand makes me get up from the table if I want more food. That gives me a chance to think and prevents me from eating more food just because it's there. I usually change my mind before I get to the refrigerator. If I really want more food, however, I have it — because I know if I leave the table dissatisfied, I'm likely to start snacking later or eat too much at the next meal.

This brings me to the next coping technique. I try never to skip a meal. People who go off in the morning without breakfast and then have next to nothing for lunch are setting themselves up to eat everything in sight in the evening. So I eat on a regular schedule every day: breakfast, lunch, mid-afternoon snack, dinner and at bedtime. This keeps my appetite under control. I never get ravenously hungry. My blood sugar stays up throughout the day, and I'm not inclined to overeat at the next meal. Strange as it may seem, I eat less when I eat five or six times a day. I believe your experience will be the same. Try it and see.

I also make it a point to eat slowly. This gives my appetite control mechanism a chance to signal my brain that I've had enough. Many people gulp their food down and that's a mistake. Take your time and you'll enjoy your food more, and be less likely to overeat.

That's another plus for the Lean-For-Life diet. It's just not possible to eat a carrot, a grapefruit or a bowl of whole grain cereal fast. You have to chew this kind of food. There's just no getting around it. And that's good because, again, it gives your appetite control mechanism a chance to work.

To make sure that I eat slowly, I always use a small spoon, plus I cut my food into pieces. For example, when I have toast or a sandwich, I usually cut it into four pieces. That makes it seem like more food — four sandwiches instead of one — and I'm less inclined to wolf it down.

Finally, I make it a point to splurge occasionally. When my wife, Carol, and I go to the movies on weekends, I have popcorn (without butter) and a big candy bar. If I feel like ice cream or pizza, I go out and have it. (It's better to eat fattening foods when you're out, because it's too easy to have seconds, thirds or worse at home.) This takes the pressure off; it keeps me from feeling deprived. I don't crave fattening food, because I know I can have it if I really want it. The truth, however, is that I don't want it very often. It'll probably be the same for you. Pig-out every once in a while, and you'll find it easier to eat right the rest of the time.

After all, eating satisfaction is the key to success. It's the Lean-For-Life way. You're happy, you don't have to count calories, and still you don't overeat. It's a win-win proposition — and a prescription for lifetime leanness.

CHAPTER V

THE EXERCISE PLAN

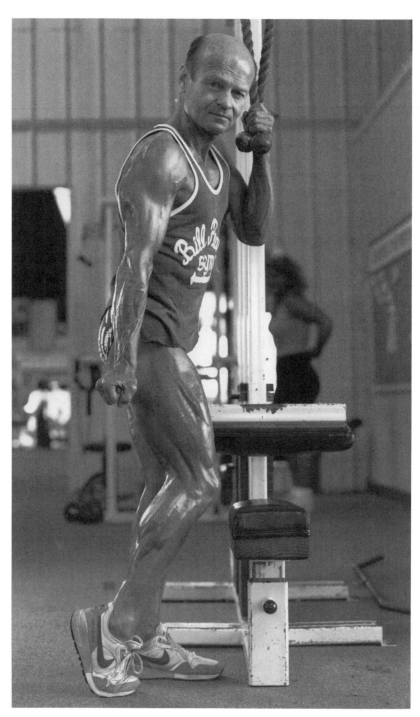

Photo by Chris Lund.

THE EXERCISE PLAN

Exercise, hopefully, isn't something you're going to do for a few months or even a few years. It's truly something you should do all your life. Indeed, exercise gets more important, rather than less, as you get older. That's what the Lean-For-Life exercise plan is: a long-term program designed to keep you training — and improving — year after year.

This exercise plan presents a balanced approach — with equal emphasis on weight training and aerobics. My other books, the *Ripped* series and the *Lean Advantage* series, basically focused on bodybuilding. Aerobic exercise (endurance training) was treated merely as an adjunct to bodybuilding, a way to lose fat and make the muscles more defined. I'm still interested in that, of course, but my focus is broader now.

Although I've been a competitive bodybuilder, I don't plan to enter any more physique contests. Nor do I plan to run any marathons. I'm not interested in either extreme. I'm interested in a balance between the two. In short, I'm interested in total fitness — strength *and* endurance. So that's what the program presented here is about — balanced fitness.

If you're like most people who exercise, or have considered adding exercise to their lifestyle, I think you'll like this approach, because I believe that people generally are interested in balanced fitness. Certainly this is a program that will benefit just about everyone. Few people can realistically expect to win a bodybuilding contest or a marathon. Just about all of us, however, can improve in both directions; we can build a more muscular, shapely body *and* develop greater endurance. And perhaps most importantly, as far as I'm concerned, such a dual approach is the best way to become lean and stay lean. That's the most exciting of all!

"Variety is the spice of life." How often we've heard that saying. Well, it's true, and my 40 years of training have taught me that it's particularly true with exercise. In fact, variety (or change) is the secret to successful long-term training. So the Lean-For-Life exercise plan includes plenty of variety — more than enough, I think, to keep you interested, challenged and improving.

Finally, the plan is goal-oriented because, to quote George Sheehan again, "A fitness program without a challenge is like an army battalion without a war." We all need a goal to give meaning to our training. As I pointed out earlier, success breeds success. Feedback, especially positive feedback, is critical; it's what keeps you interested year after year.

In summary, the Lean-For-Life training plan is long-term, balanced, varied and goal-oriented. Let's examine each of these elements and see how they combine to create a program for lifetime leanness.

A LONG-TERM APPROACH

We've all seen those ads on TV or in the print media — they usually tout a video or an exercise machine — that promise to re-shape your body in a few short weeks. They're misleading, to say the least. Crash exercise programs, like crash diets, simply don't work. If you expect quick results, you're bound to be disappointed. Dieters who demand too much of themselves — a "quick fix," so to speak — usually become discouraged and give up. The same is true of exercise. Oh, sure, you'll begin to see some changes in a

I'm interested in total fitness — strength and endurance. Just about all of us can improve in both directions. *Photo by Chris Lund.*

month or two, but to make substantial progress and develop a really great body takes time. Exercise, like winemaking, is a long-term undertaking. Runners and other endurance athletes know that. Bodybuilders know it, too.

A few years ago, I attended a national bodybuilding contest where the celebrity master of ceremonies was Sylvester Stallone's sister. If you've ever attended a physique contest, you know that there's often as much muscle in the audience as on the stage, because a lot of the spectators are bodybuilders themselves, or have friends or family who are. As Sly Stallone's sister found out, they know what a bodybuilder goes through to develop a competitive physique.

When the contestants lined up on stage, Ms. Stallone commented on their marvelous physiques, and naively added, "They've been training for this for weeks." There were a few moments of stunned silence, and then the catcalls came: "Years... years... years."

The shouts, of course, came from a few loudmouths. Most members of the audience remained silent, but I know they were thinking the same thing. It was embarrassing, because she was simply trying to give the competitors due credit for their efforts. Still, she obviously didn't know what it takes to become a national-caliber bodybuilder or a first-rate athlete in any sport. She should have asked her brother. He knows what it takes. It takes time. It takes a long-term approach.

Don't misunderstand. I'm not trying to talk anyone out of starting an exercise program — just the opposite. As I said earlier, I think exercise should be a part of everyone's life, a regular part. That's the point. A few days of punishing exercise will produce nothing but soreness and discouragement. On the other hand, a reasonable amount of exercise on a regular basis, over time, will work wonders. I have an example right here on my desk: a letter with "before" and "after" photos from a middle-aged Baltimore man.

> *A few days of punishing exercise will produce nothing but soreness and discouragement.*

"Look at the results I have achieved by your methods in only one short year," the man writes. "Many... have been amazed at the changes I have made in just this last year using your program of lifting, aerobics and eating the proper foods."

The first photo, taken in May 1990, shows him weighing 180 pounds; he had already lost 20 pounds. The second photo, taken a year later in May 1991, shows real progress; he's obviously lost more fat and his muscle tone is greatly improved.

Inspired by his progress, he is eager to continue training. "My

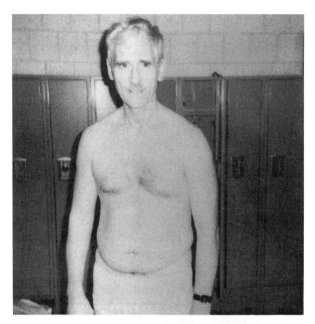

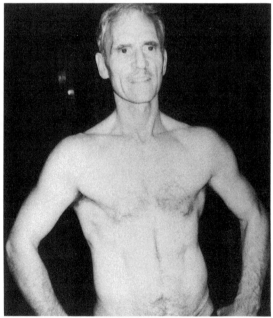

The middle-aged Baltimore man mentioned in the text is Mel Linton. These are the "before" and "after" photos he sent to me. With results such as Mel displays here — and in only one year — it's easy to understand why he's eager to continue training. *Photos courtesy of Mel Linton.*

goal," he continues, "is to be in such good shape by this time next year that I will be able to enter a physique contest and come home with a trophy in my age category."

So you see, if you take a long-term approach — as this man clearly does — exercise really works. You have to keep at it, however.

Unfortunately, if you stop exercise you lose ground fast. Research shows, according to *Exercise Physiology,* the textbook cited earlier, that a measurable decline occurs after only two weeks; after 12 weeks almost all of the training adaptations and improvements disappear. "The important point," say exercise physiologists McArdle, Katch and Katch, "is that even among highly trained athletes the beneficial effects of exercise training are *transient* and *reversible.*" Again, you have to keep training. You have to have a long-term perspective.

Some may find this disheartening. I don't, because I like to exercise. I enjoy the food I eat, and I enjoy the process of training. Training should be so rewarding and satisfying that you never want to stop. As already mentioned, enjoyment is the key; it's what keeps you training year after year. That's crucial! You must — and you can — enjoy your training. We'll have a lot more to say later about the factors that make training enjoyable. But first, let's look at the benefits, and also the drawbacks, of a balanced training approach.

A BALANCED APPROACH

The body responds to strength and endurance training differently. That's abundantly clear when you compare the physical characteristics of weightlifters and long-distance runners, for instance. Most physical performances, however, require a combination of strength and endurance.

Let's look at the physiological adaptations that take place as a result of the two types of training, and then examine how to combine the two approaches successfully. We'll find that strength and endurance training can work against each other. This happens mainly at the extremes, however. For most people and most sports, weight training and aerobics work together quite well. To be totally fit, of course, you need both. Plus, as we saw in Chapter 3, both weight training and aerobics play an important role in the fat-loss process.

My friend David Prokop, who is both a runner and weight trainer, wrote recently: "[An endurance athlete] wears his fitness primarily on the inside (in the form of a strong heart-lung system), while a bodybuilder wears his on the outside (a super-developed musculature)."

That's an easy-to-understand description of what happens as a result of the two types of training. Weight training acts primarily on your muscle fibers; it makes them bigger and stronger. Endurance training, on the other hand, works mainly on your circulatory system; it conditions the heart, lungs and blood vessels so that they can deliver more oxygen to your muscles. In addition, it brings about changes in your muscle fibers; they become more efficient in their use of oxygen as a result of endurance training.

So both types of training have an effect on the muscles. It's this overlap that sometimes causes problems, which we'll discuss shortly. First, let's look at another kind of overlap, the overlap between strength and endurance.

Endurance has a strength component. Muscle endurance depends, in part, on the strength you possess. For example, the number of push-ups you can do is correlated to the strength in your chest and arms. If you strengthen the muscles in that part of your body you can do more push-ups, because the strength required to do one push-up becomes a smaller percentage of your maximum.

By the same token, a runner or cyclist who has strengthened his or her legs through weight training will be better on hills — other things being equal — than one who relies solely on aerobic conditioning. That's one of the reasons why I was able to perform at the 99th-percentile-level on the treadmill test at The Cooper Clinic; weight training gave my legs the strength to keep going when the treadmill was at maximum incline. (For more details about my tests at The Cooper Clinic, see my book *The Lean Advantage 2.*)

Okay, you say, that makes sense, but what about the problems? For a limited number of athletes, combining strength and endurance training can be counterproductive. For example, if your goal is world-class status in Olympic lifting or the shot put, events which involve maximum effort lasting only a few seconds, then you should probably limit endurance training to interval sprints. That's because aerobic training can interfere with the development of skeletal muscle strength and power.

The reasons are poorly understood, but, as I explained in *Ripped 3,* recent research suggests that endurance training can cause a change in muscle fiber type. It seems that there exists a continuum of muscle fiber types ranging from the slowest to the fastest contracting, and that aerobic training can result in the formation of more slow-twitch fibers. There's also evidence that prolonged endurance exercise actually destroys muscle tissue. If you want more details on this I recommend that you read *Weight Training: A Scientific Approach* (Burgess Publishing Co., Min-

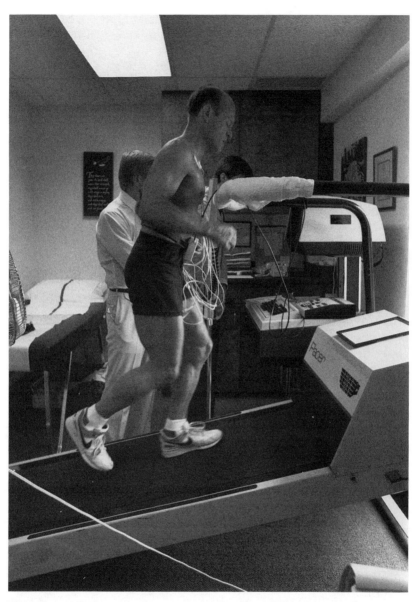

This photo shows the treadmill at maximum grade near the end of my second test at The Cooper Clinic. My time of 29 minutes — the angle increased 1% each minute to 25%, then the speed went up .2 mph until exhaustion — placed me two and one-half minutes above the 99th percentile for the 50-59 age group. It also put me in the Superior category, the top group, for men under 30. Balanced training, strength and endurance, is why I was able to perform so well. *Photo by Justin Joseph.*

neapolis, Minnesota, 1987), a book by Drs. Michael H. Stone and Harold S. O'Bryant, two of the preeminent strength training researchers in the United States.

At the other extreme, athletes who want to be elite marathoners or perhaps enter the Tour de France cycling event should probably keep strength training to a minimum. For one thing, strength training decreases capillary density because it enlarges the muscles, whereas aerobic endurance training increases it. Strength training also brings about an increase in fast-twitch fibers, while aerobic training, as mentioned earlier, results in the formation of more slow-twitch fibers.

In short, one type of training tends to cancel the other. In addition, it's only common sense that developing big muscles in the upper body will hamper a long-distance runner or cyclist; large muscles are just extra baggage to weigh them down. Nevertheless, even long-distance events have strength components (Heartbreak Hill in the Boston marathon, for example) and, therefore, some strength training is probably beneficial even for the elite endurance athlete.

As suggested earlier, however, most sports fall between the two extremes; they require a combination of strength and endurance. Wrestling, for example, requires not only strength and power but also endurance, because wrestlers continue exerting effort for a long period of time. The same is true of rowing and, of course, running events such as cross-country or the steeplechase. Most team sports (football, basketball, baseball, hockey, etc.) also require a combination of strength and endurance.

It goes without saying, of course, that both strength and endurance are required in everyday activity, such as climbing stairs, carrying luggage or — Heaven forbid — pushing your car. So, obviously, most of us can benefit from both types of training. For the majority of people, therefore, the relevant question is not whether to combine strength and endurance training, but how best to do it.

First, don't try to do too much. Overtraining is probably the greatest danger for both strength and endurance athletes. Don't compound the error by trying to do too much of *both* types of training.

As George Sheehan, M.D., wrote recently in *The Physician & Sportsmedicine* and *Runner's World,* the trend in running is now "less is more." Sheehan cites the examples of the Bare Minimum Track Club in Columbia, S.C. The runners in this club follow a program which includes a midweek speed workout, a long group run on weekends, plus one or more token runs. According to Sheehan, this is about half of what these runners were doing not long ago. "On this regimen," Sheehan says, "members have improved both marathon and 10-kilometer times dramatically."

Sheehan's own experience, going back more than 30 years, is much the same. When he started, like most runners of the time, he was a high-frequency, high-mileage runner; he ran five days a week, took a day off and then raced on the weekends. Over the years, however, he modified his program, taking more days off, running fewer miles — and adding more speed work. "Low mileage, high intensity" is how he now describes his training.

The results? His performances improved. "My 10-kilometer times are coming down, and I was recently able to run a half marathon in very respectable time," Sheehan reported enthusiastically.

Again, the trend in endurance exercise is toward less training. Sheehan sums up current thinking: "The high mileage of the past is viewed as unnecessary, and even counterproductive; it caused a significant incidence of injury and diminished rather than enhanced performance."

As detailed in *Ripped* and *Ripped 2,* my weight training experience has followed a similar path. Over the years I've gravitated toward less volume and more intensity. And, as was the case with George Sheehan, there's been noticeable improvement. Although I do not have statistics to prove it, I believe that bodybuilders today, like runners, are training less and consequently improving more.

Current research supports the belief held by both George Sheehan and me that the key to training success, more than anything else, lies in intensity. The textbook *Exercise Physiology* referred to one study, in which subjects achieved a 25% improvement in aerobic capacity after 10 weeks of training (40 minutes a day, six days a week) involving interval bicycling and running. Then, in three separate experimental trials, they reduced either frequency, duration or intensity.

When intensity and duration were maintained, but frequency was reduced to either four or two days a week, there was no fall-off in aerobic capacity. When intensity and frequency were maintained, but duration was reduced from the original 40-minute sessions to either 26 minutes or 13 minutes per day, again there was no decrease in performance.

However, reducing *intensity,* while maintaining both frequency and duration, caused a significant decline in performance level! Yes, when intensity was lowered, even 40 minutes of training, six days a week, was not enough to maintain fitness. So, in short, this study strongly suggests that training intensity plays the principal role in maintaining aerobic condition.

I know of no similar studies in the area of weight training, but my own experience and monitoring of the bodybuilding field tells

Although I do not have statistics to prove it, I believe that body-builders today, like runners, are training less and consequently improving more. *Photo by Guy Appelman.*

me that intensity is the key to maintaining strength gains as well. Quality of training, not volume, is the way to build and maintain muscle tissue.

In my view, the "less is more" principle provides an important clue on how to successfully combine strength and endurance training. High-intensity, short and infrequent workouts provide the best results in both areas. As you'll soon see, this means that even busy people will have no trouble setting up a balanced training program which will produce results.

Another clue on how to best combine strength and endurance training is found in a study described in the November 1990 issue of *The Physician & Sportsmedicine*. The question addressed was whether strength and endurance training should be done on the same day. In the same workout, subjects performed 15-20 repetitions of strength or resistance exercises for the leg muscles and eight three-minute bouts of exhausting endurance exercise on a stationary bicycle. The results for these subjects were compared with those of another group who performed strength training one day and endurance training the next.

The results? "Same-day training produced less strength gain than alternate-day training," reported *The Physician & Sportsmedicine*. The magazine also noted that there was no difference in maximum oxygen uptake and muscle endurance achieved by both groups. "These results suggest that strength and endurance training should be done on alternate days."

The magazine didn't explain why alternate-day training produced better strength gains, but I think I know. If you focus all of your effort on endurance one day and on strength the next, you can train with more intensity on both. I know, because I've tried it both ways. It's simply not possible to achieve the same level of intensity doing both strength and endurance training in the same workout.

As I explained in *Ripped 2* and *Ripped 3*, a bodybuilder who uses aerobic exercise as merely an adjunct to weight training can do both on the same day. Likewise, a person whose primary interest is running can probably do both on the same day. The reason, of course, is because the main activity can be emphasized, and the secondary activity done with less intensity.

If your objective is both strength and endurance, however, there's a problem because, again, it's not practical to train with maximum intensity for both strength and endurance in the same workout, or even on the same day.

Finally, maximum-intensity workouts should be limited to two a week. Any more than that will depress your immune system, according to Dr. David C. Nieman, Associate Professor of Health,

Leisure and Exercise Science at Appalachian State University in North Carolina. Nieman's advice is based on a study of some 2300 runners who entered the 1987 Los Angeles Marathon. In the two months before the race, approximately 40% got sick. Those who trained more than 60 miles a week got sick twice as often, according to Nieman, as those who trained less than 20 miles a week. Plus, more than 13% of those who completed the marathon were sick within a week, compared with only 2% of those who trained for the event, but didn't compete.

Why did the high-mileage runners get sick more often? Nieman said it's because high mileage depresses the activity of natural killer cells, the cells that kill foreign invaders in the body, such as viruses and bacteria. His work on a smaller group of runners showed that natural killer cell activity fell by more than 30% for almost six hours after a long, hard workout.

Nieman also had some good news. More moderate exercise, he added, actually perks up your immune system. For example, women who walked briskly for 45 minutes, five days a week, increased their natural killer cell activities. "It appears walking helps to pull the cells out of your spleen into your circulation," Nieman explained. These walkers, he said, had half as many colds as a non-walking control group.

I've gotten sick myself during periods of hard training. The last time was only a few months ago. I rarely get a cold, but I developed the sniffles twice during my preparation for the rowing competition described earlier. I wrote in my training diary: "I must be overtraining. My resistance must be down." I was doing three hard rowing workouts a week.

Train four days a week. Alternate strength and endurance workouts. Two hard, the other two shorter and less intense. The other three days, go for a walk.

Significantly, after the competition, when I reduced my hard rowing sessions to once a week, I had no more colds. So I think Nieman's advice is right on target.

Taking all of the above into consideration, I've formulated guidelines for combined strength and endurance training. They're for busy people — people who want maximum results in minimum time. That includes me, and I'll bet it includes you as well. Here, in a nutshell, is my balanced training plan.

Train four days a week. Alternate strength and endurance workouts. Make two workouts hard (one of them a strength workout and the other an endurance workout); make the other two shorter and less intense. The other three days, go for a walk.

There, you see, that doesn't sound so hard. It's a manageable

92

training plan that most people can fit into their schedule. Plus, take it from me, it works!

I'll provide more details and some variations in the chapter which outlines the actual training routines (Chapter VII). But first let's look at another key component of the Lean-For-Life exercise plan — variety.

There is no single "best way" to train. To keep making improvements you have to vary your routine. *Photo by Chris Lund.*

A VARIED APPROACH

There is no single "best way" to train. After a time the body stops responding to any program, and you hit a plateau or sticking point in your progress. To keep making improvements, you have to change your routine. This sets off new adaptation responses in the body and, presto, gains begin again!

Plus, the body can only tolerate so much stress. To prevent staleness and overuse injuries, you need to spread and redirect the stress. You also need to allow time for recovery. And don't forget fun; varied exercise routines are more enjoyable. In this section we'll examine why variation is necessary and offer tips on when and how to change your training regimen for best results.

To appreciate the need for change, it's necessary to understand how the body responds to exercise. The well-known "General Adaptation Syndrome," formulated by Dr. Hans Selye in the early 1930s, perhaps explains it best. According to Selye's theory, an athlete goes through three distinct phases of adaptation during training. The first phase, the "alarm stage," is characterized by a temporary drop in performance due to stiffness and muscle soreness. During the second stage, called the "resistance stage," the body adapts to the stress of training and becomes stronger. But if training is continued too long, then "exhaustion," the third stage, is reached. During the third stage, desirable adaptation is no longer possible. In short, after a time the body gets tired and stops responding — even to the best training program.

Olympic running champion Emil Zatopek used a marvelously descriptive metaphor to express basically the same idea. He said, "[The body] is like a spring — you press and it jumps. You press more and it jumps more. But [training] must be limited so as not to damage the spring."

In my book *Ripped 2*, I capsulized the concept this way: "Gains... can only be forced temporarily," I wrote. Then I went on to suggest a basic approach to training: "[An athlete] should push for a while, back off, and then push again." In short, I suggested a varied training approach, an approach which ebbs and flows in accordance with Dr. Selye's theory. In essence, this is the basic training model developed by Soviet sports scientist Dmitri Matveyev in the early 1960s. He called it "periodization."

Periodization forms the basis for most modern-day variable routines. In this system, training is done in cycles of gradually increasing intensity, followed by periods of lighter training. In each cycle, the type, volume and intensity of training varies. The basic idea is that you push until you almost, but not quite, reach a plateau or sticking point, and then you back off and begin again with a different training emphasis.

For example, a runner might switch from road workouts to interval training on the track. A bodybuilder might begin with light weights and high repetitions and gradually progress, in distinct periods, to heavy weights and low repetitions.

Periodization is grounded in the concept that athletes adapt better to changing stress than to constant stress. In fact, Drs. Michael Stone and Harold O'Bryant, the strength training researchers cited earlier, say that staleness and lack of progress is often the result of a "monotonous, unvarying training routine." The body grows stronger from a specific workout or set of exercises, but after a time the sheer monotony tends to tire the body so it can't respond any more. That, of course, is in line with Selye's general adaptation syndrome.

The best gains, according to Stone and O'Bryant, come when variation is introduced into the training program. This is understandable because the body has the capacity to adapt in many different ways. For example, a muscle cell has a number of different components. As Fred Hatfield explained in *Bodybuilding: A Scientific Approach* (Contemporary Books, 1984), "Each component has a specific function to perform, and by overloading that function you will force that component to develop in size or quantity — this is the way our body 'protects' itself from destructive stress. By varying the stress you will insure that maximum (muscle) growth and development is achieved."

To a bodybuilder, the two most important components of a muscle cell are the myofibrils and the mitochondria. The myofibrils are the contractile or strength components of the muscle cell, and the mitochondria are the endurance components. In order to develop the muscle maximally, you have to train both components.

Periodization in your weight training program allows you to do that very effectively as follows: At certain times you can strengthen the myofibrils by doing resistance exercises with maximum poundages and low repetitions (say, six to 10), and at other times you can use lighter weights and higher repetitions (15 to 25) to increase the size and number of the mitochondrias. Reps in the mid-range (10-15), which stress both the strength and endurance components of the muscle, can also be emphasized from time to time. It takes high reps, low reps and mid-range reps (in other words, the whole combination) to fully develop the muscle.

In the periodization system, you train in phases stressing first one part of the body and then another. You let one part rest while you stress another part. Systematic variation of this kind allows you to avoid overtraining and, importantly, keeps you improving year after year. Periodization, of course, works for both strength and endurance athletes.

That brings us to the related concept of cross-training. Cross-training or alternative training, like periodization, helps prevent overtraining and promotes total fitness.

Frank Shorter, the 1972 Olympic Marathon gold medal winner, still runs about 70 miles per week. Obviously, he enjoys running; he never plans to give it up. The problem, he says, is that "your body will only let you have so much fun." As a consequence, he's turned to cross-training. About half of his 13 workouts each week now involve something other than running. Cross-training makes it possible for him to exercise more and harder, without breaking down. Cross-training, he told *Runner's World* not long ago, "gets me to the starting line hale and hearty."

In addition to running, Shorter's routine now includes aerobic dance, cycling (indoors and out), swimming, cross-country skiing and weight training. These alternative forms of training help him maintain maximum fitness.

While the heart and lungs benefit from any form of endurance exercise, that's not true of the muscles themselves.

Ankle surgery after the 1978 Boston Marathon forced Frank into cross-training. Looking for a way to maintain cardiovascular fitness during the rehabilitation period, he turned to the stationary bicycle. Fearful of losing conditioning, he would tape his cast to the pedal and pump as hard as he could for an hour or more. To his great relief — and surprise — when he returned to running, his fitness was just about as good as before. This led him to explore, and eventually add, the other forms of exercise. He's now a strong advocate of cross-training, a true believer.

Actually, it's no surprise that cycling kept Shorter fit. "When it comes to hard training, the heart doesn't know whether the arms or legs are working," says Tom LaFontaine, Ph.D., an exercise physiologist as well as a successful Master's runner and triathlete. "The heart gets the same benefit regardless of the activity you're doing."

As noted earlier, endurance exercise conditions the heart, lungs and blood vessels. Cycling — along with many other forms of exercise — can do the job just as well as running, providing you train as hard.

You'll recall, however, that endurance exercise also brings about changes in the muscles. In fact, more than 50% of the changes take place in the muscles themselves. Endurance exercise makes each muscle cell involved a more efficient oxygen-processing and fat-burning unit. But if you want whole-body fitness, you have to train your whole body. Because while the heart and lungs benefit from any form of endurance exercise, that's not true of the muscles themselves. It's only the involved muscles that benefit.

So there are two basic reasons for cross-training. First, cross-training allows you to train your heart, lungs and blood vessels more and harder, because it spreads the stress over more of your body. "For example," Gabe Mirkin, M.D., a sportsmedicine specialist, explains, "when you run... you are stressing (primarily) the muscles of your lower leg. When you pedal a bicycle you are using your knees and hips, so you are using the muscles of your upper leg. If you alternate running and cycling, you'll be stressing different parts and allowing more complete recovery." That's why Frank Shorter is able to tolerate 13 workouts a week. If all of those workouts involved running, it's likely he'd be limping to the starting line.

Secondly, doing many forms of exercise conditions your whole body. Running and biking aren't enough, because they stress mainly the muscles of the lower body. If you want total fitness, you have to train your upper body muscles as well. That's why Shorter also includes whole-body activities such as aerobic dance, swimming, cross-country skiing and, of course, weight training. To that list you could add rowing, rock climbing and stationary cycling on a bike with a push-pull arm action. In truth, the list is practically endless. The main thing to keep in mind is that total fitness requires that you train all your muscles, upper body and lower, arms and legs.

Of course, another important aspect of a training program is recovery. The body needs time to recover. That's why training should include hard days and easy days, which is another form of variety.

The hard-day, easy-day training concept was the creation of Bill Bowerman, who coached 24 Olympians and guided his University of Oregon track team to four NCAA team championships. Bowerman, considered by many to be the father of the running boom in this country, said that every hard day should be followed by an easy day. He believed that overtraining is probably the biggest danger for both joggers and world-class runners. So he taught that a hard day should be followed by one, two, three or more easy days until the body is recovered and ready for another hard session.

Marty Liquori, formerly a world-class runner and now a television sports commentator, explained the need for easy days in his *Guide for the Elite Runner* (Playboy Press, 1980): "The idea is simply that one cannot train 110% daily and not expect to end up flat on his or her back after about five days. The body requires

The main thing to keep in mind is that total fitness requires that you train all your muscles, upper body and lower, arms and legs. *Photo by Guy Appelman.*

both the stress of exercise *and* the serenity of light days in order to grow stronger and faster."

Weight trainers, like runners, have adopted the hard/easy approach. Weight training experts Jan and Terry Todd emphasize this in *Lift Your Way to Youthful Fitness* (Little, Brown & Co., 1985): "In the research work done on periodization, and this is critical, it was found that the greatest strength increases occurred when a particular group of muscles were stressed really vigorously — maximally — only once a week. . . . This allows the body adequate rest, and you'll progress much faster than if you try to go heavy at each workout."

Remember Dr. Nieman's research which showed that training hard too frequently depresses the immune system? Nieman, as you'll recall, recommends no more than two maximum-intensity workouts each week. His research is another argument in favor of hard/easy training.

The final — and perhaps most important — reason for varied training is. . . enjoyment! "Boredom kills more fitness programs than any other villain," Jan and Terry Todd wrote in *Lift Your Way to Youthful Fitness.* "People get tired of doing the same thing all the time, whether it's working on an assembly line or running laps around a small indoor track."

Frank Shorter echoed these thoughts in his chapter on cross-training in *Runner's World Program for Peak Performance* (Rodale Press, 1987). His advice: "If it isn't fun, then don't do it." The key to a good exercise or training program, he feels, is: "Keep it fun."

I agree. In the final analysis, that's probably the best reason for a varied approach. It's simply more fun.

A GOAL-ORIENTED APPROACH

The problem most people have with exercise, as we mentioned at the outset, is staying with it. After a time they lose interest and start looking for excuses to skip workouts. It's a common and unfortunate scenario. William Evans, Ph.D. and Irwin H. Rosenberg, M.D. state in *Biomarkers,* their landmark book spotlighting the role of strength training in slowing the aging process (Simon & Schuster, 1991): "Given two athletes with similar ability and genetic heritage, it's the consistency of training that determines the extent to which one will eventually excel over the other."

Studies by Professors Evans and Rosenberg and their colleagues at Tufts University show that even 80- and 90-year old people respond to exercise marvelously well. In one study, 10 men and women, ranging in age from 87 to 96 years, *tripled* their strength as a result of an eight-week training program. So we know that exercise works. The problem, again, is motivation.

What people need, to repeat a point made earlier, is a goal to give meaning to their training. That's the secret to staying motivated. In *Biomarkers,* Evans and Rosenberg wisely devote an entire chapter to overcoming mental obstacles to exercise. "Human beings," they say, "as thinking animals, need concrete reasons for doing things — and they need tangible proof of progress." In short, you need to be goal-oriented, and you need positive feedback. Without those critical elements (i.e., a meaningful goal and tangible progress), most people eventually give up and stop training altogether.

The reasons why people train, of course, are as varied as the people themselves. Your reason is probably different from mine. What's more, the reasons why we train change over time.

My training goals certainly have evolved over the years. They're different now than they were when I started training in my teens. I've been training for so long now, about 40 years, that it's second nature to me. A lifestyle without regular exercise, for me, is almost unthinkable. My training has become part of my self-image. You might say it's ingrained in my psyche. As I wrote in *Ripped 2,* it's part of what allows me to say, "I'm okay." It's more than that, however.

Training gives me a feeling of control — control of my body and my life. I understand exercise. It works for me. When I train, I'm in control. This quote from boxer Sugar Ray Leonard says it all as far as I'm concerned; "A lot of time, out of training, I don't even know where I am. Training gives me sanity. That's the one time in my life when I know what I'm doing."

The wonderful thing about training is its predictability. You can count on it. If you work hard, smart and consistently, you get results. Training has always been my most reliable source of success. Again, it gives me a sense of control. I think you'll agree that's important these days in a world where so many things seem beyond our control. "The hour or so I spend in my gym calms me for the rest of my day," I said in *Ripped 2,* and that statement still holds true for me almost 10 years later.

As I get older, however, and more aware of my mortality, my training has taken on a new significance. I never noticed before, but when I look around today, my age-group peers seem to be growing old at an accelerating pace almost before my very eyes. Their hair seems to be turning gray, even white, practically overnight — and their waistlines just grow. I'm sure it's mainly my perception that has changed. What's really true, however, is this:

With each year that goes by, the gap widens between those of us
who exercise and take care of ourselves and those who don't.
Photo by Chris Lund.

With each year that goes by, the gap widens between those of us who exercise and take care of ourselves and those who don't. That gives my training a new sense of urgency.

My doctor, Arnie Jensen, the preventive medicine specialist I've mentioned before, assures me that I can do more for myself than he can. I know he's right. As Evans and Rosenberg say in *Biomarkers,* "You're largely responsible for your own health throughout your whole life...."

That becomes all the more true, of course, as you age. If you want to stay out of the clutches of the health care system as long as possible, you have to keep exercising and eating right. Drs. Evans and Rosenberg, both experts on aging, urge that we heed the words of Ern Baxter, who wrote a book called *I Almost Died* about his recovery from a mid-life heart attack. He wrote, "If your lifestyle does not control your body, eventually your body will control your lifestyle. The choice is yours."

> **The more accurately you define the meaning training has for you, the more successful your training is likely to be.**

So that's why I train. Now it's up to you to decide the *real* reason why you train or want to start. The more accurately you define the meaning training has for you, the more successful your training is likely to be. Make sure your goal is one that you can articulate and define. ("Because it's good for me" is too general.) You need tangible proof of progress. You need positive feedback, if possible, in each and every workout.

Note what Arnold Schwarzenegger said in a recent issue of *Interview* magazine about the five-hour-a-day training sessions he used to do when he was the world's greatest bodybuilder: "People say, My God, you [were] so disciplined. But it had nothing to do with discipline; I loved it. Because I knew that every time I went to the gym I was one step closer to winning the competition."

Arnold's regimen is different now — one hour a day, less weight training and more cardiovascular work — because his goals have changed. Now that he's an actor, he doesn't need to be as big as when he was competing for the top title in professional bodybuilding, Mr. Olympia. But he still needs to stay in shape for his movie roles and to serve as an example for the youth of America in his position as Chairman of the President's Council on Physical Fitness and Sports. Nevertheless, you can bet that he still gets satisfaction from each workout.

You should make it a point to do so, too. Do your best to make every training session a positive, enjoyable experience. Structure your training to produce a feeling of accomplishment. An important part of each workout should be setting realistic and attainable goals for the next session. Nothing complicated is required;

while the workout is fresh in your mind, just take a few moments to think about what you can realistically expect to do next time. The idea is to set yourself up for a positive experience in the next training session.

Ideally, you should make progress — lift a few more pounds, do a few more reps, run or cycle a little faster or longer, etc. — in each workout. But don't get caught in the trap of thinking *you have to improve with each workout*. Again, you want to make each training session a positive and enjoyable experience. Don't make training an ordeal. That means you should usually save a little something for the next workout. Like Arnold Schwarzenegger said, you want to get a little closer to your goal each workout. Still, it's best to take your time. If you push to the absolute limit every workout, you'll have the encore problem. In other words, you'll think to yourself, "How can I top that." That will discourage you from going back into the gym or out on the track the next time.

So the trick is to set a goal, a realistic goal, and try to make steady — but slow — progress towards that goal each workout. When you reach the goal, i.e., hit your peak, back off. Don't beat your head against the wall, so to speak. Rather, when you reach your limit, take a break; then set a new goal.

In *Biomarkers,* Evans and Rosenberg remind us of the need to constantly update goals. "Sustained motivation in any endeavor comes not from achieving a particular goal, but rather, from striving for that goal. Once a goal is reached, the average person experiences a letdown, even depression, kind of postpartum blues. The only cure is to find a new goal, a new challenge, and start the process of mastery all over again."

Read that quote again, because it's right on. George Sheehan imparted the same message when he wrote, "Happiness, we come to discover, is found in the pursuit of happiness." And psychologist and philosopher William James, in his treatise *Is Life Worth Living?*, written way back in 1897, put it this way: "Need and struggle are what excite and inspire us; our hour of triumph is what brings the void."

Summing up, therefore, here's how to stay motivated: Find a training goal that excites and inspires you; work hard, and when you reach the goal, find a new goal — and then start the process all over again. Follow that pattern and your training will never be boring. It'll be stimulating and challenging. You'll move from one success to the next. And if my experience is anything to go by, you'll love it!

CHAPTER VI

THE EATING PLAN
IN ACTION

Photo by Guy Appelman.

CHAPTER VI:
THE EATING PLAN IN ACTION

ABOUT THE MEALS

Many people come to our office in Albuquerque for help with their diet and exercise problems. In the course of a day-long consultation, I usually invite these visitors to my home for breakfast and lunch. I prepare both meals in their presence, explaining each ingredient as I go along. When we sit down to eat, I tell them the benefits and drawbacks,if any, of each item on the menu. In other words, I tell them *why* the meal we are sharing will make and keep them lean. I explain where Carol and I shop for the food and suggest variations they might like to try. There is no better way than this, I've found, to illustrate the Lean-For-Life eating style.

On the following pages I'll use essentially the same method to demonstrate the eating plan in action. But beyond simply looking at breakfast and lunch, we'll also talk about a mid-afternoon snack, dinner and a bedtime snack. What's more, the meals we'll be discussing have been carefully selected to convey the most important aspects of the Lean-For-Life eating plan. First, I'll explain the ingredients and preparation of each meal, just like I would if you were in the kitchen with me; then I'll tell you how each meal embodies the principles of the eating plan, just as I would if you were sitting across the table from me.

The meals described here represent an eating style, a manner of eating, not a diet.

As I emphasized in Chapter Three, it's not enough to know *how*. I believe you need to know *why* the eating plan works. If you understand the basic underlying principles, you'll be ready to plan your own meals and menus, not just for the next week, but for the rest of your life. That's what I want you to be able to do, create your own meals, meals you'll be comfortable with... yes, forever.

In a departure from the typical diet book, the meals presented here do not include a calorie count. That's because this isn't "a diet book." As I pointed out earlier, diets don't work. They just make you miserable. People soon go back to eating the foods that made them fat in the first place. The meals described here represent an eating style, a manner of eating, not a diet.

I keep track of my body fat level by weighing myself and measuring my waist each morning. *Photo by Guy Appelman.*

I rarely count calories. Instead, I focus on the kind of food I eat. I suggest that you do the same. If you select the right kind of food, you can eat until you're full and satisfied *without getting too many calories!*

While I don't count calories, I do keep track of my body fat level. I weigh myself and measure my waist each morning. The waistline is an especially good indicator. If it starts expanding even a little, you know your body fat is increasing. When I see that happening, I adjust my food intake. That doesn't mean I start counting calories, however. That's not necessary. I simply adhere more closely to the diet plan explained in Chapter Four and further illustrated in this chapter. When we talk about the meals, I'll explain how I "clean up" or tighten my diet from time to time. That approach is painless and it has never failed me. I'm confident that it will work for you as well.

I should alert you, however, that in the course of explaining and analyzing the meals, I may give the calorie count for certain foods. That's not meant to encourage calorie counting, however. It's simply to convince you of the validity of the eating plan, to make you a believer.

Before I share the first meal with a visitor during my consultation, I often take the person food shopping. That gives me a chance to explain or review the basic principles of my eating style. You and I should pause at this point to briefly review those principles as well.

In the supermarket, my wife and I basically stick to the outside walls where the fresh fruits, vegetables and dairy products are located. The only time we venture over to the inner shelves is when we're looking for beans, rice and whole grain items. Of course, we go to the frozen food section to get frozen fruit and vegetables. Generally, we steer clear of most packaged and refined foods.

The basic idea is to eat foods that fill you up and make you feel satisfied without exceeding your energy needs. That generally means that you should emphasize low-fat, high-fiber foods and avoid calorie-dense foods. Stick to whole foods the way they are grown — with nothing added or removed. Avoid foods that have the bulk and fiber removed, and sugar or fat added. Those are the foods that give you a lot of calories in a small volume and encourage overeating. In other words, try to eat foods in Mother Nature's wrapper.

In addition, Carol and I go easy on animal products, because they're usually high in fat and contain no fiber. However, we do use low- and nonfat dairy products for complete protein and nutritional balance. As explained earlier, we also use lean meat, fish or chicken in small amounts — for flavoring — because eating enjoyment is important. You should never leave the table hungry or feeling dissatisfied.

Okay, enough theory, let's get to the meals that show the Lean-For-Life eating plan in action.

BREAKFAST

1 cup cooked whole grains (oats, rye and barley)
1 cup skimmed milk (½% fat)
1 chopped apple
1 orange, cut into bite-sized pieces
1 handful berries (strawberries, blackberries, raspberries or blueberries)
2 tablespoons of protein powder

Ingredients and Preparation

Whole grains, of course, are a perfect example of a food that you buy just the way it comes in nature. The only thing removed is the inedible outer covering. A wide variety of whole grains can be

The basic idea is to eat foods that fill you up and make you feel satisfied without exceeding your energy needs. *Photo by Guy Appelman.*

found in most health food stores, and many supermarkets are now stocking them as well.

I mix hulled oats, whole rye and pearled barley, then cook them together. This is my favorite mixture, but any whole grain or combination of grains is fine. Experiment with various grain combinations and see what you like best.

Whole grains can be cooked in a big pot on the stove; just add water and follow the instructions on the package. I fixed grain this way for years; it takes about 45 minutes. Now, however, I use an automatic rice cooker, which makes the process much easier. You simply pour in the grain, add water and turn it on; when the grain is done, the cooker turns itself off. Your part, setting up and putting things away afterward, takes about five minutes. The cooker does the rest.

Carol and I purchased ours at an Oriental cooking supply store, but any well-stocked store that carries cooking appliances should have an automatic grain or rice cooker. I suggest that you buy the large size, so you can prepare enough for a week or more and store it in the refrigerator. With the right equipment, you'll find whole grains only a little more trouble to prepare than corn flakes.

This breakfast can be eaten hot or cold. I usually mix one tablespoon of protein powder with the precooked grain, pour the milk on top and heat in the microwave for about three minutes. The fruit will already be at room temperature because I take it out of the refrigerator the night before. While the microwave is taking the chill out of the milk and grain, I use the time to prepare the fruit. And when I take the grain and milk out of the microwave, I add the fruit to the heated mixture and sprinkle another tablespoon of protein powder on top.

Be sure you use skimmed milk. As noted earlier, the calories in milk are mainly in the milkfat. Whole milk contains 3.5% fat and about 60% more calories than the skimmed variety (150 calories vs. 90). Most supermarkets, as you probably know, also carry "low-fat" milk. But there's a substantial difference between that product and nonfat or skimmed milk. Low-fat products contain an intermediate level of fat, usually 1 to 2%; they contain fewer calories than whole milk but more than skimmed milk. Always read the label carefully.

The protein powder I use is our own brand, Ripped Milk & Egg Protein/Vitamin & Mineral Powder Concentrate. As the name suggests, it contains vitamins and minerals as well as protein. Our protein powder adds a great deal of nutritional value, but what I like best is its creamy texture and sweet taste (it also contains fructose). Protein powder, of course, is optional. You can skip it entirely, or use a low-calorie sweetener such as Equal. Personally, I like the idea of a nutrition-packed sweetener such as our protein powder. If you use another brand of protein powder, make sure it tastes good and contains no fat.

Any fruit which is in season can be substituted for those shown. Other fruits I use from time to time are bananas, pears, peaches, nectarines, grapes and cherries. Any fresh fruit that suits your fancy is fine. When fresh berries are not available, you can use the frozen variety — make sure it has no sugar added. Simply add the frozen berries to the grain and milk before heating in the microwave; frozen berries thaw in a jiffy.

For a special treat, add half an ounce of raisins or sunflower seeds, or a few whole almonds. Go easy on these items, however, because they're concentrated-calorie foods, i.e., they contain a lot of calories in a small volume. (When I need to tighten my diet, concentrated-calorie items like these are the first thing I reduce or eliminate.)

Whole grains, which come in a package like this, are available in many supermarkets and almost all health food stores. An automatic cooker makes grain preparation almost as easy as cornflakes. *Photo by Guy Appelman.*

A Perfect Example

This breakfast is an almost perfect example of the Lean-For-Life eating style.

It contains practically no fat; there's one-half gram in the milk and a little in the grain. If you add sunflower seeds or almonds, of course, you'll add fat — and calories. Nuts and seeds, as noted earlier, are loaded with calories. I reserve sunflower seeds, almonds and raisins for special occasions, and even then I only add them sparingly.

Natural carbohydrates make up the bulk of this meal. The grain and fruit are whole foods, nothing has been added or subtracted. Almost all the ingredients in this meal are exactly the way they come in Mother Nature's wrapper. The only exceptions are the milk and protein powder, which are refined products.

Fat has been removed from the milk but, unlike the case with most refining, that's a positive alteration. The protein powder, of course, is a concentrated food; it contains no water or fiber. What it does contain, however, is desirable; it adds a few grams of complete protein and, equally important, provides texture and flavor. At an addition of only 35 calories per tablespoon, I think you'll agree that's a bargain.

This breakfast, of course, is near-vegetarian. Skimmed milk is the only animal product of consequence, and it serves an important nutritional function. Aside from the protein powder, milk is the only source of complete protein in this meal. One cup of skimmed milk contains about nine grams of high-quality protein. That's important because it balances the incomplete protein in the grain and fruit (yes, there is a little protein in fruit). As you'll see, I make it a point to include a source of complete protein in every meal or snack. Plus, milk contains a significant amount of Vitamin B-12 and calcium, essential nutrients often lacking in a vegetarian diet.

I have this cereal for breakfast almost every morning. I've had it (or some variation) a thousand times or more, I guess, and I never seem to tire of it. I always serve it to our visitors — and have yet to find a person who doesn't like it. The only complaint I've ever had is: "I just can't eat this much." (The portions shown are what I eat; adjust them up or down to suit your appetite and body size.)

While we're discussing breakfast, let me take the opportunity to remind you again not to skip meals. Paradoxical as it may seem, eating regular meals keeps you from overeating. Your appetite stays under control because you never come to a meal ravenously hungry.

It's especially important that you not run off in the morning without breakfast. A primary reason is the energy your brain needs to function best. As I explained in *The Lean Advantage 2*, the brain exclusively relies on glucose (blood sugar) for energy. If your blood glucose level falls, the brain cannot function properly. The glucose to supply your brain comes first from the sugar contained in your circulating blood, but this source only provides about 20 grams of glucose, which doesn't last long. Next, the brain takes the glucose stored in your liver — a maximum of about 70 grams. The glucose in your blood and liver is enough to tide your brain through the night, but that's about it. When you get up in the morning, your brain needs a new supply of glucose. If it doesn't get it, you're apt to feel sluggish and shaky; you definitely won't be operating at top efficiency. So when you get up in the morning, do your brain a favor: eat a good breakfast.

The most important feature of my breakfast cereal, in addition to the nutritional value, is its volume. It takes a big bowl to hold this cereal. Every time I cook up a batch of grain I'm reminded why there's so much volume here — and yet not many calories.

The most important feature of my breakfast cereal, in addition to the nutritional value, is its volume. It takes a big bowl to hold this cereal. In fact, our visitors often complain: "I just can't eat this much." *Photo by Guy Appelman.*

Even though I've cooked it literally hundreds of times, I'm always amazed to see the grain soak up more than twice its volume in water (I use six cups grain and 12 to 15 cups water). I look at the grain covered with all that water and say to myself, "No way." Nevertheless, when I remove the cover an hour or so later, there's no water in sight, only cooked grain!

So cooked grain, like the human body, consists largely of water. The same is true, of course, with fruit, the other main ingredient in this cereal. That's why there's so much volume and so few calories in this breakfast; the bulk of it is water. And that's why it fills you up — satisfies you — before you take in too many calories.

Stomach-filling volume without excess calories is characteristic of the Lean-For-Life eating style.

Stomach-filling volume without excess calories is a characteristic that typifies the Lean-For-Life eating style. It's the main reason why a low-fat, natural-carbohydrate, near-vegetarian diet keeps you lean.

As stated in the report of the physicians' group quoted earlier, the type of food included in this meal "can be consumed with impunity." Stick to meals such as this breakfast, and you'll be able to eat practically all you want without getting fat. (Additional breakfast suggestions can be found in my book *Ripped 3*.)

*****

Cooked grains, of course, can be used in many other ways. For example, you can create a dinner dish by replacing the fruit in this recipe with steamed vegetables. Whole grains go well with beans. I prefer most cooked grains to rice because they are chewier. Grain can be substituted for rice in casseroles. And they can be added to soups and salads or simply eaten as a side dish (like rice) with any meal. Use your imagination.

LUNCH

Almond Butter Sandwich:
  2 slices whole wheat bread
  Almond butter (roasted, nothing added), spread thin
1 cup yogurt mixture:
  ½ cup plain, nonfat yogurt
  ½ cup skimmed milk
  1 tablespoon low-sugar jam or jelly
1 grapefruit, cut into wedges

Ingredients and Preparation

Any kid can make a nut butter sandwich, of course, but adult weight watchers might appreciate a few construction tips.

Carol and I buy our bread at a health food store which has a better selection of whole grain breads than our regular supermarket. My favorite is a high-fiber, wheat-bran bread made by Food For Life Baking Company (Corona, Calif.) called Bran For Life. This bread has nine times the crude fiber content of standard white bread and 19% fewer calories. What I like best about Bran For Life, however, is its delicious nutlike flavor. It's really chewy and goes great with peanut butter or almond butter. (The supermarket where Carol and I shop now has a separate nutrition section which stocks part of the Food For Life bread line, too. So look around the next time you shop for groceries; you may be surprised what you find.)

Remember the Michigan State University study in which overweight college students ate 12 slices of high-fiber bread every day and lost weight? You can't go wrong eating bread. Any whole grain bread will do just fine. Pick the one you like best. By all means check the label for calorie content, but don't let that be your only selection criterion. Try them all and, again, select the bread that tastes best to you.

The almond butter I use contains nothing but roasted almonds; it has no added sugar, salt or oil. Carol and I also purchase this item at a health food store; but we've noticed recently that our regular supermarket carries "nothing-added" peanut butter (no almond butter yet).

As readers of my earlier books know, peanut butter used to be my favorite. Lately, however, I've come to prefer almond butter. It spreads more easily (thinner) and I've decided it tastes better, too. You'll also find sunflower seed butter, sesame seed butter, cashew butter and perhaps others at your health food store. I urge you to try them all.

The yogurt mixture is something new for me as well. In the past I used straight yogurt, but recently I got the idea for this yogurt mixture, and I like it a lot. It goes better with an almond butter sandwich (like peanut butter and jelly). I stir a tablespoon of low-sugar jelly into a half-and-half mixture of plain, nonfat yogurt and skimmed milk. I eat it with a spoon when I'm having the sandwich.

This is my version of flavored yogurt. It only contains about 110 calories per cup. That's excellent because the flavored, low-fat yogurt available in stores often contains as many as 240 calories per cup.

The calorie content of yogurt varies from brand to brand. So be sure to check the label. The plain, nonfat yogurt I use is made by Alta-Dena Dairy (City of Industry, Calif.); it contains only 90 calories per cup. Carol and I first discovered this yogurt at our health food store, but it's now available at our supermarket as well. Other brands of nonfat yogurt, I've noticed, contain 130 calories or more per cup. "Low-fat" yogurt, like low-fat milk, contains more fat and calories.

Low-sugar jelly is another item Carol and I discovered recently at our regular supermarket. The version we use is put out by Smucker's and comes in a wide variety of flavors (apricot, strawberry, red raspberry, Concord grape, blackberry, orange marmalade, etc.). They're all delicious and contain half the calories of the regular variety (eight calories to the teaspoon vs. 18 for regular jellies and jams).

I started eating grapefruit when Jim Harvey, a friend who owns a citrus grove in Cocoa, Fla., sent me a crate full of grapefruit and oranges. I never used to like grapefruit; I thought it was too bitter. But Jim's gift changed my mind. The grapefruit he sent me were wonderful! Citrus fruit is now a regular part of my diet. I usually have a whole grapefruit with lunch (I cut it into wedges and eat it with my fingers). And, as mentioned, I like oranges cut bite-size on my breakfast cereal. Citrus fruit, as you probably know, is a rich source of Vitamin C and bioflavonoids.

Don't Deny Yourself

Remember the Manhattan lawyer who, after losing 143 pounds on a liquid formula diet, hired a car and driver and went on a 22-stop, crosstown eating binge? He demonstrated the truth of Jeneen Roth's perceptive comment: "For every diet there is an equal and opposite binge." His mistake was denying himself food that he really wanted. This nut butter sandwich is my guarantee not to make the same mistake.

As I wrote in *Ripped 3,* there's a strong psychological component to eating: "It's human nature to crave what you can't have, and craving usually spells doom for dieters." That's why I have an almond butter sandwich for lunch almost every day, even though I know nut butter is loaded with calories (1 ounce of almond butter, about two tablespoons, contains 190 calories). I like almond butter; that's why I eat it regularly.

I know that in the long run I'll do better and consume fewer calories if I cut myself some slack, so to speak, and have what I enjoy for lunch. I don't get carried away, however; I eat almond butter — and other high-calorie foods — only in measured amounts. I spread a thin layer on my sandwich, and then I put the jar back in the refrigerator *before I sit down to eat.* That's important.

As stated earlier, that's my number one calorie-control technique. I plan each meal and only put on the table the food I intend to eat. For high-temptation items like almond butter, that's crucial! If I leave the jar in full view on the table, I'll probably be tempted to stick my finger or spoon back in for more — even though I don't *really* want more. So putting the container away as I do might be considered a kind of balancing act. I eat enough almond butter to satisfy me, but I use my put-everything-away-first trick to keep me from going overboard.

I strongly recommend that you follow my lead. Don't deny yourself a favorite food or foods. That will only make you crave the item more. Have a measured amount on a regular basis. That way you'll stay satisfied, in control — and lean. Remember, put the extras away — before you sit down to eat.

You've no doubt noticed that I eat the same thing for breakfast and lunch most days. That's another calorie-control technique that has served me well for more than a decade. My book *Ripped,* published in 1980, contains a section called "Uniformity Makes It Easy," which explains why I eat basically the same thing almost every day.

Remember, put the extras away — before you sit down to eat. Don't leave food in full view on the table to tempt you unnecessarily. *Photo by Guy Appelman.*

Varying my food intake every day would make it harder to keep track of how much I eat. Like a scientist conducting an experiment, I can control what's happening to my body better if I'm consistent in my eating.

When I eat basically the same thing every day, I know that my calorie intake is on an even keel. This, in turn, keeps my weight level; equally important, when my body fat creeps up, as it does from time to time, it's easy to make the necessary adjustments.

As mentioned earlier, I almost never count calories. When my weight and waistline — and the mirror — sound the alarm that my fat level is rising, I review my eating pattern, and then make a few simple adjustments. I look for places to tighten up my diet. I start measuring my food more carefully. (Yes, I measure my food. That's part of uniform eating.) I trim the little "extras" that may be sneaking in. For example, I make sure I have a level, rather than a heaping, cupful or tablespoonful of things. I take care to

I weigh or measure most of the food I eat. That's part of uniform eating. *Photo by Guy Appelman.*

When your fat level starts creeping up, the key is to make small but regular adjustments in your diet, subtle cutbacks that your fat cells notice, but you don't. Take it from me, this works! *Photo by Guy Appelman.*

spread the almond butter on my lunchtime sandwich thinly, rather than thickly. I cut back on fattening treats, such as raisins or sunflower seeds, and I'm more careful about my snacks.

Eating basically the same thing most days makes tightening up here and there easy. By contrast, the adjustments would be much more complicated if I ate different foods every day. I wouldn't know where to start. The real problem, however, is that I might cut back too severely and make myself uncomfortable or even desperate — like the Manhattan lawyer.

I urge you to strongly consider following a uniform eating pattern. At first blush, I realize, eating the same thing most days may not seem appealing to you. However, you may find it's not bad at all, especially if you chose meals that you really like — this almond butter lunch, for example.

If you still prefer to vary your diet, go ahead; just remember that you'll have to spend more time planning your meals. (Personally, I don't have time to do that.) Make sure you eat foods that fill you up without giving you too many calories — the kind of food we've been discussing. And when your fat level starts creeping up, cut back on concentrated-calorie foods that contain a large number of calories in a small volume. Look for places to clean up your diet — without making yourself miserable.

As mentioned earlier, this form of adjustment has never failed me. The key is to make small but regular adjustments, subtle cutbacks that your fat cells notice, but you don't. Try it; you'll see what I mean. It's effective — and painless.

Again, these calorie-control techniques are very important. Don't deny yourself foods you really want, even fattening foods like peanut butter or almond butter. Put the "extras" away before you sit down to eat. And although it's not mandatory, uniform eating makes it easier to keep your food intake — and fat level — on an even keel. Take it from me, these things work!

Plus, combined with the Lean-For-Life eating style, they make calorie counting a thing of the past.

(If you need more lunch suggestions, please consult *Ripped 3*.)

MID-AFTERNOON SNACK

1 piece of fruit (any kind)
1 cup skimmed milk
1 slice whole grain bread

Don't Starve and Stuff — Snack

Snacks have gotten a bad rap. The general public has the idea that snacks are fattening.

I remember seeing Jack LaLanne a few years back whip up a health food drink of some kind on television. Rather than taste the concoction himself, he handed it to an assistant with the comment, "I never snack between meals."

I admire Jack LaLanne. He was advocating fitness and healthful nutrition long before it was the thing to do. Now over 70, he still practices what he preaches. He's probably the most enthusiastic fitness proponent on earth. Still, I disagree with him on snacking between meals. The truth is that snacking on the right kind of

Do what I usually do: have a mid-afternoon snack of whole, natural foods. *Photo by Chris Lund.*

food keeps your appetite under control. It actually helps you stay lean.

As I have written before, nutritionist Nancy Clark, author of *The Athlete's Kitchen* (Bantam Books, 1983) has the right idea. She believes that planned snacking is better than the "starve and stuff" routine. Many people hit a valley of fatigue, so to speak, at about mid-afternoon. Their blood sugar drops. They feel tired. They need something to eat. Trying to hold out until the evening meal is a mistake.

What happens when you resist the urge to snack? You overeat at dinner. That's why I have a mid-afternoon snack almost every day. My snack carries me though the rest of the afternoon, and I'm only moderately hungry at dinnertime. Occasionally I get busy in the afternoon and don't stop for a bite to eat. Boy, can I tell the difference when I get home! I have no patience. I grab anything and everything I can find, and stuff it down. My normal control temporarily vanishes — and that's definitely bad for my waistline. On days when I skip my snack, I almost always end up eating more than usual.

It's easy to see how snacks got a bad name, of course. When people think snacks, they don't think fruit, milk and bread. They think candy bar and soda pop. Snacking on foods like that, of course, probably will make you fat.

Remember the experiment described by Jane Brody involving apples, applesauce and apple juice? The subjects given apple juice experienced rebound hypoglycemia; their blood sugar shot up and then, a short time later, dropped to an abnormally low level. They experienced hunger much sooner than the subjects who ate the whole apple.

I had a similar experience recently, only worse. Carol and I were driving back to New Mexico from California where our son Matt goes to college. We had been on the road for several days and were anxious to get home. We stopped for lunch on the final day, but didn't stop again until we needed gas late in the afternoon. I was hungry, so I bought an ice cream bar and a package of M&M candies at the gas station. I knew that was a bad idea, but we were in a hurry and I needed a pick-me-up.

Well, I paid for my lapse of judgment that evening. By the time we got back to Albuquerque, I felt like my blood sugar level was down around my ankles. I felt awful! I had to steady myself and concentrate hard just to drive the car. (Our brain, you'll recall, needs glucose to function properly.) Well, we made it home. But, predictably, I really blew it then. I ate my fool head off for the rest of the evening.

I should have had the foresight – it would have been easy – to take along some fruit, vegetables and bread to snack on in the car. Had I done that I would have been fine. My blood sugar would not have fallen, and when I finally got home I would've been only moderately hungry — and in control.

I hope I learned my lesson, and that you benefit from my experience as well. Do what I usually do: have a mid-afternoon snack of whole, natural foods.

DINNER

Vegetable Stew with Beef:
    1 baked potato, chopped into bite-sized pieces
    4 ounces frozen mixed vegetables (broccoli, red peppers, bamboo shoots and mushrooms)
    2 ounces frozen corn or peas
    2 ounces extra-lean ground beef (raw weight)
    2 tablespoons green chile salsa (no sugar or oil added)
    1 cup water
2 slices whole grain bread, toasted
2 tablespoons low-sugar jelly or jam

Ingredients and Preparation

I bake the potato separately in the microwave — one minute per ounce of raw weight. Potatoes, like bread, are good diet food. If you stick with the plain potato — no butter or sour cream — it's practically impossible to overeat.

As you might imagine, we use the leanest ground beef we can find. Carol buys it at a local meat market. It's marked "extra lean" and very little drainage fat appears after it's cooked. Carol makes patties in two-ounce serving size, puts them in individual plastic sandwich bags, and then freezes them for later use. I put the patties in the microwave directly from the freezer, sandwich bag and all. They cook nicely in a little over a minute.

My son scolds me for using frozen vegetables. A purist, he buys his fresh. I usually don't have time to wash, chop and cook fresh vegetables. So I take advantage of the wonderful variety of frozen vegetables now available at supermarkets. (The nutritional difference between frozen and fresh vegetables is minimal.) I always check the label to be sure no sugar, oil or sauce is added. I want vegetables only — no extras. (A little added salt is okay.)

The vegetable mix shown in this recipe is one of my favorites. I love the crunchiness of the bamboo shoots. Broccoli, the other main ingredient, is loaded with nutrients, including three grams of protein. At only 7½ calories per ounce, it also provides a great deal of bulk and chewiness. President Bush's aversion to broccoli

I use meat — in small amounts — to add flavor. *Photo by Chris Lund.*

notwithstanding, that's a real deal. Oriental-style vegetables is another of my favorites (French-style green beans, cut broccoli, onions, red peppers and mushrooms). You can find these and many other great combinations at your grocery store.

As indicated in the recipe, the corn or peas are also frozen. I don't bother thawing the vegetables. I add them to the baked potato and cooked beef directly from the freezer. I spoon on the salsa (my favorite is Old El Paso Thick 'N Chunky) and then pour about a cup of water over the top. The water spreads the flavor throughout the dish.

Finally, I put the whole shebang in the microwave until piping hot. That usually takes about six or seven minutes.

The bread and low-sugar jelly are the dessert in this meal. Pick any whole grain bread you like. The low-sugar spread is the same as mentioned earlier. Pick your favorite flavor. I like them all.

A Little Meat'll Do Ya

Do you remember that slogan, "A Little Dab'll Do Ya," in the old Brylcreem hair tonic commercial? Well, the same goes for beef and other flesh foods, including fish and fowl.

Americans typically use meat as the main course. As mentioned earlier, I believe this is a mistake. Not only is meat high in fat and low in fiber, there's good evidence that man wasn't made to eat meat. I know for a fact that my bowels function better without meat. Nevertheless, like most people, I enjoy the taste of meat. So I compromise. I use meat — in small amounts — to add flavor. This meal is an example of that compromise.

A mere two ounces of beef literally makes this meal. Without the added beef, it would be a pretty bland affair. With the beef, however, it's a feast.

And there's another reason to include meat in your diet occasionally. It's one of the best sources of iron. The iron in meat (including fish and fowl) is absorbed twice as efficiently as that in vegetables. Plus, meat in the diet makes the iron from other sources more usable.

Iron deficiency is one of the most common nutritional problems worldwide. The iron in meat is heme iron. The iron in vegetables is nonheme iron. The body can assimilate about one-third of the heme iron consumed, but barely 10% of nonheme iron is assimilated. Again, the high-quality iron in meat allows the body to use the low-quality iron in vegetable foods better.

To avoid iron deficiency anemia, commonly known as iron-poor blood, it's probably wise to eat some meat. That's especially true for athletes. When there's an iron deficiency, muscles lack sufficient oxygen and, consequently, they fatigue more quickly.

The salsa in this recipe, like the beef, serves as a taste enhancer. Being from New Mexico, I prefer green chile salsa. The salsa I use also contains diced tomatoes, diced onions, diced jalapeños, salt, onion powder, garlic powder, distilled white vinegar and natural flavor. It contains no sugar or oil and, therefore, has very few calories. Pick any salsa that suits your tastebuds. Just remember to check the label for ingredients such as sugar and oil that add unnecessary calories.

Like fruit and whole grains, vegetables—with nothing added or subtracted— provide volume and eating pleasure with very few calories.

The only drawback to a sauce like this is added salt. But, as noted earlier, a little salt is not a problem for most people; few of us are "salt sensitive." If you have high blood pressure or simply don't know what your health situation is, check with your doctor.

As I said earlier, vegetables are a key component of the Lean-For-Life diet. This meal graphically illustrates why.

Believe it or not, four ounces of the vegetable mixture included in this recipe contains only 30 calories! By comparison, two ounces of frozen peas or corn contain about 40 calories. So the volume-to-calorie ratio of this mixture is terrific! Like fruit and whole grains, vegetables — with nothing added or subtracted — provide volume and eating pleasure with very few calories. They fill you up without filling you out.

This entire meal, including the bread and jelly, provides less than 600 calories. That's amazing when you consider that a double cheeseburger, fries and a chocolate malt give you about 1,500 calories!

*****

Use your imagination to create many variations of this dinner recipe. To illustrate, here are two more suggestions; these meals also provide less than 600 calories:

Vegetable Stew with Tuna:
    1 cup cooked grains (same as breakfast recipe)
    8 ounces frozen broccoli, corn and red peppers
    2 ounces water-packed tuna (diet style with very low sodium)
    1 heaping teaspoon Butter Buds powder (a low-calorie, butter-flavored mix available in supermarkets everywhere)
    1 cup water
2 slices whole-grain raisin bread

Place grain, vegetables, tuna and Butter Buds in a bowl and mix well. Add water, and heat in microwave for about seven minutes or until piping hot.

Serve the raisin bread for dessert.

Chicken (skinned and boned) can be substituted for the tuna in this recipe. Simply cook a few ounces of chicken separately in the microwave. Make sure that the chicken isn't underdone, however; chicken is sometimes contaminated with salmonella bacteria, and must be cooked thoroughly to ensure that this organism is destroyed. As you know, microwave ovens often undercook in spots, so rotate the chicken while it's being cooked.

Vegetable Stew with Cheese Sauce:
 1 cup cooked brown rice
 8 ounces frozen western-style vegetables (potatoes, green beans, onions and red peppers)
 ¼ cup tomato sauce
 2 ounces mozzarella cheese, shredded
 ½ cup nonfat yogurt
 ½ cup water
1 peach sliced into bite-sized wedges

Precook the rice according to the instructions on the package. Place the rice and vegetables in a bowl. Make cheese sauce by combining the tomato sauce, shredded cheese and nonfat yogurt; mix well. Add cheese sauce to the rice and vegetables, then stir. Add water, and heat in the microwave for about seven minutes or until all ingredients are hot.

Serve the peach for dessert. When fresh peaches are not available, try frozen peaches with no sugar added. Peaches, like most fruits, are very low in calories; one medium peach contains only 38 calories and 3.5 ounces of frozen peach slices contain 45 calories. So you can eat your fill of peaches (fresh or frozen, no sugar added) with no worry whatsoever. That's not true of the cheese in this recipe, however. Two ounces of mozzarella cheese provides 170 calories. And most other cheeses are even higher in calories!

At any rate, you now have some working examples of how to create satisfying, low-calorie — but filling — meals for your dinner table. Other suggestions can be found in *Ripped 3*.

BEDTIME SNACK

½ cup Post Grape-Nuts or 2 shredded wheat biscuits
1 sliced banana
1 cup low-fat buttermilk (sweetened)

Ingredients and Preparation

I discovered recently that I like buttermilk when Carol brought a quart home for baking purposes. When I'm around, nothing in the refrigerator is safe. I took a sip or two, then a glassful, and found to my surprise that I enjoyed the taste of buttermilk. Plus, the nutritional information on the carton made me like it even more.

Despite its name, buttermilk is made from low-fat or skimmed milk. One cup typically contains about 100 calories. It has a buttery, thick texture, but only one or two grams of fat per cup. Because of the tart flavor of buttermilk, most people will probably find it more palatable with Equal or some other low-calorie sweetener added. The low-sugar jelly mentioned earlier also does the trick. Sweetened buttermilk is like having your cereal topped with cream — except you don't get the extra fat and calories. It's like having your cake and eating it, too!

Soy milk or beverage is another cereal topping you might like to try, especially if you have an intolerance for milk and other dairy products. It's made from soy beans, a high-quality source of vegetable protein, and contains no lactose, the ingredient in milk which disagrees with some people. You'll find soy drink in health food stores and at your supermarket. It comes in regular and low-fat varieties, as well as several flavors (plain, carob, vanilla, etc.). Read the label carefully, however, because some soy beverages are high in fat and calories. But if you look around, you'll be able to find soy beverage that has only 1% fat, which means you'll be getting a product that gives you only a few more calories than skimmed milk or low-fat buttermilk, and tastes good poured over cereal and fruit, or consumed all by itself.

In addition to the ready-to-eat cereals listed above, I also suggest you try cooked oatmeal with sweetened buttermilk or vanilla soy drink (1% fat) poured over it. Add one cup water to one-half cup dry rolled oats (regular, not instant) or oat flakes and place in the microwave; in about two minutes, the oatmeal will be ready.

Packaged foods are usually processed: fiber is removed, sugar or fat added, creating less volume and more calories—a combination that insures overeating.

Topped with a sliced banana and buttermilk or soy milk (1% fat), the calories in all three cereals (Grape-Nuts, shredded wheat and oatmeal) total less than 450.

Good Things in a Box?

As a rule, I avoid eating anything in a box. Packaged foods are usually processed; the fiber is removed and sugar or fat added. That means less volume and more calories, a combination that practically insures overeating. Still, a few good things do come in a box. Post Grape-Nuts and shredded wheat are two such products. They are the exception, however.

More than half the dry weight of some packaged cereals is

sugar. An analysis published by the U.S. Department of Agriculture showed that many of the cereals purchased by Americans contain 20% or more sugar by weight.

In ancient times, man's preference for sweet foods served him well; it helped him identify when foods like fruits and berries were ripe and ready to eat. When the sweetness comes from added sugar, however, a sweet tooth no longer works to our advantage. According to *Jane Brody's Nutrition Book*, "Newborn rats will consume sugar water in preference to a nutritious diet, even to the point of malnutrition and death." Sugar boosts sales for food companies. Unfortunately, it boosts the size of our waistlines as well.

Post Grape-Nuts and shredded wheat contain no added sugar or fat. All the sugar in these cereals occurs naturally in the grain.

I make it a practice to never buy a packaged food without checking the ingredients and nutritional information on the label. *Photo by Guy Appelman.*

According to the USDA survey, Grape-Nuts and shredded wheat contain 7.0% and 0.6% sugar by weight respectively. Grape-Nuts, because it contains more natural sugar, has a few more calories than shredded wheat (110 versus 80 per serving).

High fiber content is another reason why these cereals are relatively low in calories. Shredded wheat is a little better on that score as well — two servings, the portion-size in this snack, contain six grams of dietary fiber versus four for Post Grape-Nuts.

So some foods acceptable to weight-conscious people do come in a box. Not many, however. I make it a practice to never buy a packaged food without checking the ingredients and nutritional information on the label. Shredded wheat is "100% natural whole wheat." The Grape-Nuts box says, "No Sugar Added, No Fat Added." Nothing is added to either product. That's the formula for leanness.

Plan It!

George Sheehan says, "For me, obesity starts at 6 p.m." That's true, of course, for many people. By early evening, the most active part of the day is over; they're home with the TV and the refrigerator. One snack leads to another. As I remarked in *The Lean Advantage,* "From the standpoint of time on your hands and the availability of food, the evening hours are dangerous." Still, I almost always eat something at bedtime — for the same reason I have a snack at mid-afternoon: so I'm not ravenous when the next mealtime rolls around.

My bedtime snack is planned, however. I usually know exactly what I'm going to have. I look forward to it. And I'm not tempted to eat anything else.

In other words, my bedtime snack helps me control my evening food intake. Plus, I sleep better on a full stomach. Hunger pangs don't get me up during the night to raid the refrigerator. (Again, you'll find more snack suggestions in *Ripped 3.*)

*****

There you have it — a full day of eating the Lean-For-Life way! It's a practical, easy-to-understand approach which takes into account not only your physical needs, but your often overlooked psychological needs as well. Put the good, old-fashioned common sense embodied in these few simple recipes to work for you. Master the Lean-For-Life eating style. Make it your own. And you'll be on the road to a lifetime of eating pleasure — and leanness. *Bon appetit!*

CHAPTER VII

THE EXERCISE PLAN IN ACTION

Photo by Chris Lund.

Photo by Guy Appelman.

CHAPTER VII:
THE EXERCISE PLAN IN ACTION

NAVIGATING THE ROUTINES

Exercise, more than diet, is really the greatest weight regulator. My friend David Prokop, who edited this book, has been a serious long-distance runner for more than 35 years. He estimates that during that time he's run more than 90,000 miles! He stays slim because he exercises so much, not because he diets. In fact, to sustain such an exercise regimen, he eats far more than any sedentary person ever could — even the most overweight individual. Dave once wrote: "I've estimated that if I ate all the food I've eaten over the years and never run a step, I'd weigh 2700 pounds today!"

We're not for a moment suggesting you need to exercise to the same extent that Dave does in order to stay slim. But exercise is really the eye of the needle we all have to go through to stay slim *and* healthy. The exercise routines presented in this section will enable you to do that easily and comfortably, although some dedication — obviously — is required.

I hope you'll be as excited about these exercise routines as I am. The result of a 40-year evolution in my training, they are the best I've ever used. They keep me motivated... and they work! Plus, they require only four hours a week, and they're fun. What more could you ask?

Still, there's a problem. This section is practically a book in itself as far as length is concerned. So from a purely logistical point of view, there's a great deal of information for you to read and digest. To the best of my knowledge, no other book describes training sessions in such detail. Readers who already train seriously will, I believe, relish the day-to-day discussion of the intricacies of each workout. That may not be true, however, for people relatively new to training — or certain aspects of training. People with limited experience may be somewhat repelled or frustrated by the detail found here; they may feel overwhelmed or even frightened. I don't want that to happen, because exercise is too important to your health — and your waistline. So, let me take a few moments at this point to reassure and encourage people in that category and help them successfully navigate their way through the routines.

The first thing to
keep in mind is
this: Exercise is
the most
important factor
in becoming and
staying lean.

The first thing to keep in mind is this: exercise is the most important factor in becoming lean and staying that way. As a practical matter, it's almost impossible to control your body fat level without regular exercise. As I wrote in *Ripped 3,* "Your body tends to mirror your lifestyle." Leanness depends, to a large extent, on your level of activity. As we discussed earlier, diet alone has a notoriously poor record in keeping fat off. To lose fat and keep it off requires a three-pronged approach: diet, aerobics and weights. The bottom line, therefore, is that the key to body fat control is *regular* exercise.

The "regular" part is where most people fail, and that's where these routines — or, more importantly, the exercise principles embodied within them — can help you the most. If staying motivated is a problem, as it is for all of us from time to time, I can assure you that the detailed guidance provided in this section will help — no matter what your level of experience.

Remember Dr. Mihaly Csikszentmihalyi (or Dr. C, as we called him) and his formula for staying motivated? Dr. C, the author of *Flow: The Psychology of Optimal Experience* and one of the world's foremost authorities on motivation, says the secret to staying motivated is to take control of an activity and "cultivate it in the direction of greater complexity." Well, that's an important feature of these routines. They illustrate how to stay motivated — for a lifetime! — by cultivating your exercise program in the direction of greater complexity.

It took many years, of course, for my exercise program to evolve to the point described here. And I realize that most readers are probably not as far along the exercise path as I am. That's really not a problem, however, because you don't need to be advanced to benefit from what I have to say. You can simply take as much — or as little — from each routine as you want or your situation warrants. What's more, everybody (beginner and serious athlete alike) can benefit by understanding how these routines reflect Dr. C's formula, and why following the principles of flow will help you stay motivated.

In short, I believe that just about everyone will learn something of value in reading about the Lean-For-Life exercise routines. Even if you decide not to do any of the routines, you'll probably gain new insights on the subject of motivation, and how to make exercise — and therefore leanness — a permanent part of your life.

There's something else you should know before we continue. The routines described here utilize some fairly sophisticated aerobic exercise machines. The equipment used is found in home gyms and fitness centers everywhere, but it's not inexpensive. The routines are designed to help you get the best results from the best equipment on the scene today. After all, this is the age of computerized training. People are lining up across the country to use high-tech exercise machines. In my opinion, if you have access to this type of equipment, as I do, you should use the equipment in the very best way possible. That's one of the things this book can help you do. Nevertheless, I realize that some readers will not have access to such equipment. If that's your situation, does it mean the information in this chapter is irrelevant to you?

No, not at all. You can benefit from these routines even if you're like my editor, David Prokop, who doesn't even own a warm-up suit. Dave's philosophy is: "Give me some shoes, give me a pair of shorts, give me a road, and get out of the way!" He's been training all his life, and that's how he prefers to operate. No fancy machines, no frills. Since he lives in southern California, the land of endless summer, he says he doesn't need a warm-up suit.

But even a hard case like Dave can use the information in this chapter. For example, he could convert the motorized treadmill workouts offered here into running or walking workouts. And you can do something similar with all of the machine workouts. (Any bike — stationary or otherwise — can be substituted for the Schwinn Air-Dyne, and any rowing machine will work fine in place of the Concept II Rowing Ergometer.)

Again, the thing to focus on is the underlying training principles involved in each program. Please remember that the most important thing is not so much the specific details of the routines, but rather the underlying principles. Don't overlook the forest because of the trees.

And what about complete beginners? For example, can an out-of-shape beginner jump right into the weight workouts? Frankly, I wouldn't advise it. A beginner shouldn't "jump" into any exercise program. Nevertheless, what I have to say in this chapter can save novice lifters a lot of grief. They can get a leg up, so to speak, on how to get started by studying the training principles explained here. Plus, there's a special section called "Help For Beginners." It has some words of encouragement — and caution — for people new to training, along with tips on how to get started properly.

Finally, let me suggest a possible way to approach this lengthy section on the Lean-For-Life exercise routines: read it through once, fast, to get a general idea of the routines; as you scan the pages, focus on the basic principles illustrated. Then go back and study the routines and sections that interest you most. Lastly, if you decide to use some or all of the routines, you can consult this chapter before each workout. It will be just like having me right there by your side.

And one last thing before we begin. Remember the promise I made to you in Chapter Two? Let me repeat it: stick with me to the end, and I promise that you'll be well rewarded. That promise still holds. Yes, I know the length and depth of this section will require some effort and study on your part, but isn't that true of anything really worthwhile?

Okay, now that we have that out of the way, let's continue. I think you're going to enjoy these routines as much as I do.

About The Routines

These routines, of course, are the Lean-For-Life exercise plan in action. They illustrate the long-term, balanced, goal-oriented approach we talked about earlier. You'll notice that there's an equal emphasis on weights and aerobics. Also, the routines are designed to provide you with a constant challenge. The focus is on progression; the intensity increases from week to week. And there's tremendous variety in these routines; every training session is different. These are the type of routines that keep me interested — and lean — year after year. I believe they'll do the same for you.

Each routine covers a period of 12 weeks. I tell you what to do in detail, day by day and week by week. But that's not because I want to encourage a "by rote" approach to training. On the contrary, my main objective is to help you understand the principles underlying the routines. As was the case when we discussed meals, I want you to focus more on *why* than *how*. If I accomplish my purpose, you will be able to create routines geared to your own special needs — routines that will keep you training and progressing year after year.

With that goal in mind, I'll start by explaining how the routines are structured and presented — and why. As outlined in Chapter Five, the routines call for four training sessions a week, two days for weights and two for aerobics. In general, half of the workouts are relatively hard and the other two are somewhat easier. As mentioned, each routine covers a 12-week training cycle.

The training cycles are divided into phases of four weeks or less. With some variation in the more advanced routines, volume is high at the beginning and decreases from phase to phase; intensity, on the other hand, begins relatively low and increases. As you'll soon see, in the first routine the changes in volume and intensity are relatively subtle to accommodate the needs of people less experienced in exercise. The second and third routines, however, are geared more for the advanced person who, in order to progress, requires higher initial volume and intensity, and more

These are the type of routines that keep me interested — and lean — year after year. I believe they'll do the same for you. *Photo by Guy Appelman.*

frequent change. This, of course, complies with the flow formula; the added complexity in each succeeding routine keeps you challenged and interested.

What's more, the routines also are designed to take fullest advantage of what we've been taught about training by Dr. Selye's General Adaptation Syndrome. You'll note there's an ebb and flow in volume and intensity. You push for a while, back off, change course, and then you push again. In this way, your performance escalates gradually from phase to phase, and you end each cycle a little stronger, fitter and probably leaner than before.

As you'll see, this is a wonderful and satisfying way to train. Done properly — and that's important — you almost never hit what we call a sticking point in your progress. You experience one success after another. As explained earlier, that keeps you motivated. Success breeds success.

Another enjoyable — and important — feature of these routines is that each training session only lasts about an hour. Many bodybuilders and endurance athletes, I realize, train longer. Nevertheless, in my experience, the ideal length of a workout is about 45 minutes to an hour. You can stay focused and maintain intensity for about that period of time. Go longer, however, and you lose interest; you begin to merely go through the motions, so to speak.

Moreover, there's a scientific basis for keeping training sessions relatively short. As you may know, Bulgaria has fielded the world's best Olympic weightlifters in recent years. Ivan Abadjiev, formerly the Bulgarian national coach, made sure his lifters trained no longer than 45 minutes at a time. The reason, he told touring members of the U.S. Strength and Conditioning Association, is that 45 minutes is the length of time the human male can maintain a maximum testosterone secretion level. I can't prove it, but my body tells me that the Bulgarians are on the right track.

(Interestingly, Abadjiev had his lifters train for 45 minutes *six times a day*. I can't argue with the performance results of his athletes, but my body and my mind won't let me go along with him on this concept of six-times-a-day training. It may work for gifted, young athletes with unlimited time to train — for a while anyway. Nevertheless, most people, even if they had the time and inclination, would be destroyed — physically and mentally — by such training. Their motivation would evaporate in no time flat.)

Also, in keeping with the less-is-more philosophy, the weight routines include only one set of each exercise after warm-up. Many bodybuilders will consider that practically heresy, I know. Traditional wisdom calls for three to five sets, or more, for each exercise. And that may be necessary for novices, but for the experienced weight trainer who really knows how to concentrate and push to the limit, one set is all that's required. A recent experience convinced me of this... again!

I've never been one to do very many sets. I don't like doing the same exercise over and over. I find it boring. Nevertheless, for a change, I was doing three hard sets per exercise in a recent workout cycle: 12 reps with a medium poundage, eight with a heavy weight, and a final back-off set of 20 repetitions. I had been increasing the poundages on all three sets for several weeks. So I thought I was performing close to my limit on all three sets. Then, one day, I decided to do only the first set and forego the other two sets. The result was eye-opening!

After a few easy warm-up sets, I loaded the bar with the weight I thought was my 12-rep maximum for this particular exercise, the

For the experienced weight trainer who really knows how to concentrate and push to the limit, one set is all that's required. *Photo by Guy Appelman.*

deadlift. But when I reached 12 reps I was still going strong, so I continued. I did 13, 14 and, finally, I ground out 15 repetitions!

So how is it I was able to do 15 reps when I previously was only able to do 12 with the same weight on the first set? Note that this set of deadlifts was done at the same place in my workout as before. Because the deadlift is a difficult exercise involving essentially the whole body, I usually do it first. Moreover, this was my first work set after the warm-up. So I was fresh at this point — in both workouts. So it wasn't that I was tired in my earlier workouts. No, the difference was more subtle. It was psychological.

Obviously, in my earlier workouts, I was holding back on the 12-rep set. Whether I knew it or not, I was pacing myself. Subconsciously, I was saving my energy for the two sets to follow. However, when I cut back to one set, I could focus totally on that set without thinking about the sets to follow. That freed me to make a better effort; it produced a more intense and, therefore, a more productive set with the result that the next day I was sore in all the right places.

Soreness is Mother Nature's way of telling us we have pushed our muscles harder than usual. The technical term is "delayed onset muscle soreness." It is caused by microscopic tears in our muscle cells. The tears cause inflammation and swelling, and therefore pain. Within limits, such soreness is a good sign. It indicates that the complaining muscles are adapting, getting stronger in response to exercise.

That, after all, is what training is all about — exercise physiologists call it "progressive overload." It's the key to success in all forms of exercise, strength and endurance. By pushing our bodies beyond that to which they are accustomed, we force positive adaption. Our muscles get stronger, bigger and more enduring.

As explained in Chapter Five, intensity (more than frequency or duration) is the key to progress in training. So, it stands to reason — doesn't it? — that one intense set is better than many sets where you are holding back and pacing yourself.

Intensity, of course, is the measure of how hard you are working in an exercise. Intensity is relative. It relates to the capacity of the individual. A performance that is very intense for one person may be easy for another. In the routines offered here, intensity is indicated differently for weight workouts and aerobic sessions. Let's clarify that now so there will be no confusion later.

In the weight routines the number of repetitions is shown along with a percentage figure. The percentage indicates how near you are to maximum for that number of repetitions. For example, if 12 repetitions with 100 pounds is your limit, then 100 pounds would be 100% of your 12-repetition maximum. The percentage figure refs to your personal best. So 85 pounds would be 85% of your 12-rep maximum, for example.

The point is that the actual weight you use will be unique to you. In the routines you are given the number of repetitions and the intensity is expressed in the form of a percentage. You may have to experiment a little, particularly on new exercises and repetition ranges, but you'll soon find your current maximum poundages.

Your maximum, of course, is a kind of moving target; it will change. As you continue to lift, you'll become stronger in each exercise. That means, of course, that 100 pounds will no longer be your 12-repetition maximum. Slowly but surely, you'll be able to do 105 pounds for 12 reps, then 110 and so on. Again, that's what training is all about — progressive resistance and improvement. When you exceed your previous best, you simply adjust your training poundages accordingly.

In aerobic sessions, I usually go by "perceived rate of exertion." In other words, I judge the intensity level of my workout on the basis of how I feel. *Photo by Guy Appelman.*

In aerobic exercise, heart rate is a standard measure of intensity. That's because heart rate increases linearly with oxygen uptake and exertion level; the harder you work, the faster your heart beats. The intensity level in aerobic workouts is often expressed as a percentage of your maximum heart rate. That can be misleading, however, because maximum heart rate is quite variable.

For many people, the standard formula for estimating maximum heart rate — 220 minus your age — doesn't work very well. For instance, by that gauge, my maximum heart rate should be 166 (220 - 54 = 166). My maximum heart rate, however, as measured on a treadmill at The Cooper Clinic, is actually 183. I regularly achieve a heart rate in excess of 166. So, unless you have it measured, rather than estimated, percentage of heart rate maximum may not be a reliable indication of the intensity of your aerobic exertion.

For most people, "perceived rate of exertion" works better. What this means is that you go by how you feel. Experiments have shown that, with a little experience, people can judge their heart rate based on their perceived level of exertion. That's what I usually do, and that's what I suggest you do in these routines.

(It isn't my intention, however, to discourage the use of heart rate monitors. I know from personal experience that the chest strap monitors distributed by Polar USA, Inc. perform flawlessly. If you know your maximum heart rate and have access to a good monitor, then, by all means, use the monitor. Perceived rate of exertion is suggested as the guideline in these routines simply because most people don't know their true maximum heart rate.)

The level of intensity in the aerobic workouts offered here ranges from "very easy" to "very hard." In addition, I give you the equipment settings or readings I use to achieve that intensity level. On the treadmill, for example, the angle I use is indicated as a percentage of grade, and I also give you the speed in miles per hour. On the Schwinn Air-Dyne, a stationary bicycle with push-pull arm action, you're given the speed as indicated on the dial. And on the Concept II Rowing Machine, I'll give you the 500-meter pace as shown on the electronic performance monitor. The settings and readings from the equipment, of course, are personal to me. For example, an angle and speed on the treadmill that is "very hard" for me may be only "somewhat hard" for you, or the reverse may be true. Nevertheless, I'm sure you'll be able to zero in quickly on what's the appropriate angle and speed for you when you do the actual routines.

I should also mention that the weight training equipment used in these routines is the equipment Carol and I use. It's nothing fancy, just standard equipment found in most well-equipped home gyms. Still, I realize that you may not have access to all of the equipment used in the routines. Again, that's not really a problem.

Ideally, of course, it would be best if you have access to a wide range of weight training equipment, since that would give you greater variety and make your training sessions more interesting. Still, it's not essential. A great deal can be accomplished with even the most basic weight equipment most people have available: a barbell, dumbbells, a bench and squat racks.

So, again, don't worry if your equipment is limited. Focus on the training principles underlying the routines. Remember, the most important thing is to understand *why*. Once you master the basic ideas behind the routines, you'll have no trouble adapting the routines to the equipment available to you.

Now, as promised, let's pause for a few words of advice to beginners.

Help For Beginners

I realize that beginners and those getting back in shape after a long layoff will probably need extra help to get started. I have encouraging news for people in that category. Plus, I want to give you some excellent information sources and a few words of caution.

Beginners, in a manner of speaking, have a great advantage. They have what I call a "virgin body." Their low starting level as far as fitness is concerned gives them a greater upside potential. A beginner's body isn't accustomed to the stress of exercise and, therefore, responds readily to even slight changes in activity level. William Evans, Ph.D., and Irwin H. Rosenberg, M.D., the Tufts University professors who authored *Biomarkers,* agree: "Research shows that the single best predictor of how much gain an individual will make during an exercise program is his or her baseline fitness."

The key is to start slowly, and gradually incorporate exercise into your lifestyle. Don't bite off more than you can chew. Take a long-term approach. With exercise, as in most pursuits, slow and steady wins the race. Here are some tips to help you get started on a sound footing.

Lawrence E. Lamb, M.D., author of the highly respected *Health Letter* (900 Haddon Ave., Ste. 326, Collingswood, N.J. 08108), says that everyone — children, young adults, men and women — should have a health and physical status evaluation before beginning an exercise program. The American College of Sports Medicine says it's especially important for people over 35 to have a medical exam. If you have any medical problems, of course, it's mandatory that you consult your physician before starting an exercise program. But even if you have no known problems, it's probably a good idea to get checked out by your doctor anyway.

I was fortunate in that I always had a doctor on call from the very beginning. My late father was a physician. I always was able to pick up the phone and consult with him on practically a moment's notice. Frankly, until he passed away a few years ago, I didn't fully appreciate how lucky I was. My Dad always had a ready ear for my complaints. For this reason — and many, many others, of course — I miss him greatly.

If you don't have a sports-minded physician on call, consider having a complete medical and fitness evaluation at a sports-oriented hospital or clinic. As noted earlier, I've been checked out twice at The Cooper Clinic in Dallas, Texas, the first time when I turned 50, and the second a year later. These evaluations of my health and fitness were extremely helpful. After poking and prodding my body for a day and a half each time — and running me to exhaustion on the treadmill — the people at The Cooper Clinic pronounced my overall condition "superb." It was great to have

Dr. Kenneth Cooper congratulated me for achieving an aerobic fitness rating of "superior" for men of any age. The Cooper Clinic also pronounced my overall health "superb." *Photo by Justin Joseph.*

their stamp of approval on my lifestyle. The sense of assurance that comes from such an evaluation is well worth the time and cost involved. (I'm planning to go back to The Cooper Clinic later this year for a recheck. My goal is to be better at 55 than I was at 50.)

As we said earlier, a complete newcomer to weight training will find many tips throughout this book on how to get started properly and, just as importantly, how to keep going once he/she has started training. In fact, most of the basic information needed by someone who has never lifted weights before — warm-up and cool-down, general exercise performance, the principle of overload, the importance of rest, etc. — is found on these pages. About the only major thing not included are instructions on how to do standard weight training exercises, such as those included in the weight

> *As I have already suggested, beginners and out-of-shape people must ease gradually into both strength training and aerobics.*

workouts. We didn't cover that information because it's readily available elsewhere. For example, most weight training sets come with an instruction booklet containing workouts for beginners and descriptions of the basic exercises.

What's more, the bodybuilding magazines which are available on every newsstand (*Muscle & Fitness, Flex, Ironman, MuscleMag International, Muscle Training Illustrated* and others) frequently include articles for beginners and photos illustrating the performance of basic exercises. A beginner might also find it worthwhile to sign up at a local fitness center for a month or two of basic weight training instruction.

If you find that you do need extra help, there are a number of excellent books for beginners. Here are a few that I think you'll find especially helpful:

Weight Training for Beginners (Contemporary Books, 1982) was written by Bill Reynolds, formerly editor-in-chief of *Muscle & Fitness,* the world's leading bodybuilding magazine. Bill now holds the same position at *Flex,* another bodybuilding magazine published by the Weider Company. As the title suggests, this book is for people just getting into weight training. It covers all the basics: terminology, equipment and exercise technique. The focus is on simple free-weight (barbells and dumbbells) training routines.

A similar book for beginners who are older is *Post Middle Age Power* by Loren Taylor (D. Nakii Enterprises, Albuquerque, N.M., 1986). Unhappy with himself physically, Loren started pumping iron at age 62. He ended up a few years later stronger, healthier and looking better than he had in his youth. *Post Middle Age Power* is the book Taylor needed, but couldn't find, to help him get started. I wrote the foreword to this book and recommend it to beginners of any age, but especially to those who take up lifting late in life.

Lift Your Way to Youthful Fitness (Little, Brown, 1985) is a bigger and more comprehensive book (339 pages) written by Jan and Terry Todd. As mentioned previously, Terry is a former editor of *Strength & Health* magazine. He and wife Jan, both formerly world-class lifters, are perhaps the pre-eminent scholars of the iron game, both past and present. Their book includes the most painstaking and thorough advice for beginners to be found anywhere.

Keys to the Inner Universe by bodybuilding legend Bill Pearl, a four-time Mr. Universe winner, is an encyclopedia of bodybuilding. It weighs five pounds and has more than 600 pages. Pearl, an inspiration to bodybuilders everywhere, is now in his 60s, but still trains six days a week and retains his superb physique. His book has the most complete list of weight training exercises assembled anywhere. Every piece of equipment and every exercise imaginable is included with drawings and explanatory text. To give you an idea of the detail, 93 pages are devoted to exercises for the triceps, the three-headed muscle on the back of the upper arm.

Finally, I want to again call your attention to *Biomarkers* (Simon & Schuster, 1991) by Evans and Rosenberg, professors of nutrition and medicine at Tufts University. It's long been known that aerobic exercise helps to keep us young. This landmark book presents dramatic evidence that strength training may be even more important in retarding the aging process. Evans and Rosenberg say the two most important biomarkers — signposts of vitality that indicate one's physiological age — are muscle mass and strength. They're the lead dominoes, so to speak. When your muscle mass and strength start to topple, the other indications of aging soon make their appearance. Preserve your muscular strength, however, and the rest of you will hold up as well. Aerobic exercise and diet are important, but strength training, according to Evans and Rosenberg, is pivotal if you want to stay young longer.

You should read *Biomarkers* for the ground-breaking research information it provides, but I also recommend it for another reason. As I have already suggested, beginners and out-of-shape people must ease gradually into both strength training and aerobics. "Start *slowly* and increase the vigor and duration of your activity as your fitness improves," advises the American Medical Association. *Biomarkers* tells you exactly how to do that.

In addition to a chapter on basic exercise concepts, Evans and Rosenberg provide a 16-week catch-up program for relatively

Bill Pearl, author of *Keys to the Inner Universe,* was the Arnold Schwarzenegger of the 1960s. This photo of him in a Eugene Sandow pose shows why. *Photo by Leo Stern courtesy of Bill Pearl.*

unfit individuals and a 12-week program for the moderately fit. Surprisingly sophisticated, these programs tell you what to do on a day-by-day basis; they start you out walking on day one and bring in strength-building exercises for the upper and lower body a week or so later. They introduce you to such concepts as split training, and even incorporate the hard-day/easy-day training principle.

In short, if you want day-by-day instruction on how to get in shape for the routines in this book, you'll find it in *Biomarkers*. Don't waste your time with homemade weights, however, despite what *Biomarkers* says. The makeshift equipment described in *Biomarkers* simply won't provide the variation in resistance needed for serious progressive weight training. Invest in a set of adjustable weights (a barbell and dumbbells) and a sturdy exercise bench and squat rack.

> **To continue progressing, you must change the stress and your routine more frequently.**

All of the books mentioned above and many others are available from Ripped Enterprises. Call or write for our recommended book list.

An Overview: The Big Picture

Variety, as mentioned at the outset of this section, is a key component of this exercise plan. Planned variation is really what makes these routines work. You'll notice that three routines are presented here, and the main difference between them is the rate of change. In the first routine, volume and intensity change every four weeks. These variables change every two weeks in the second routine, and in the last routine they change weekly.

This is important because the longer you train, the faster your body adapts to the stress of exercise. To continue progressing, you must change the stress and your routine more frequently.

You'll also note that each routine is divided into three basic phases, which are repeated one or more times. The main difference between the phases is the relative proportion of volume and intensity. The endurance phase is the first phase; it's high in volume and low in intensity. The second phase, the strength and endurance phase, is moderate in both volume and intensity. Finally, there's the strength phase, which is high in intensity and low in volume.

In the weight training workouts, the weight lifted and the number of repetitions are varied to change the intensity and volume of training. In the aerobic sessions, speed (or angle of incline) and time are the variables involved.

The way this actually works in practice is that during the

endurance phase, relatively light weights and high repetitions (about 20) are used in the weight training sessions. Similarly, the aerobic sessions during the endurance phase emphasize interval training with relatively slow-speed (or low incline) 10-minute work periods. In the strength and endurance phase, moderate weight and repetitions (about 12) are used in the weight training sessions, and in aerobic sessions, speed (or incline) is increased and work periods are shortened to five minutes. Finally, in the strength phase, intensity is high (e.g., heavy poundages and fast or hard work periods) and volume is low (about 8 reps and one- or two-minute work periods).

As you can see, volume and intensity are inversely related. Like a teeter-totter, when one goes up the other goes down. It works essentially the same in aerobics and weight training. When you lift a heavy weight or run fast, you simply can't continue very long; you're forced to do fewer repetitions or reduce the time and distance of your run.

Now we're about ready to move on to the actual routines. But one suggestion before we do that, however: please read everything we have to say about these routines. That's because the explanations often have application beyond the particular routine involved. For obvious reasons, I do not repeat myself in every routine. For example, in the first routine, we explain the general warm-up and cool-down at the beginning and end of every training session. After that, the warm-up and cool-down are simply listed without further comment. So even experienced athletes are urged to read the description of the routines from start to finish; if you jump around, reading only bits and pieces, you may miss relevant and helpful explanations.

THE A-B, WHOLE-BODY BALANCED ROUTINE

Now let's put the concepts we've discussed into action. As the name says, this routine is balanced. That is, the whole body — arms and legs, upper body and lower — is trained aerobically and with weights. In addition, this is a periodization routine. It utilizes the hard-day/easy-day training principle. The flow formula is applied; the feedback is always positive. You never encounter the encore problem (of thinking, "How will I top that?") because, in each phase, a goal is set and achieved slowly but surely — and then you move on to the next phase. Finally, this routine — like all the other routines — has a lot of variety, which makes it fun.

Let's start with the weekly schedule. In terms of day-to-day sequence, it's the schedule we'll use in all the routines.

Day 1: Weight Workout A — hard
Day 2: Treadmill — hard
Day 3: Walk
Day 4: Weight Workout B — easy
Day 5: Air-Dyne — Easy
Day 6: Walk
Day 7: Rest

You'll notice that in this and the other routines, I've numbered the training days rather than using days of the week. In my own training, Day One always falls on Monday. I realize, however, that's probably not convenient for everyone. Therefore, I've used numbers so your training week can begin on Saturday or any day that suits you best. A good plan is to schedule the two hard sessions, Day One and Day Two, on the days of the week when you'll have the most time and energy to train.

You will notice that there are two different weight workouts, A and B. Both workouts involve the whole body. When the whole body is trained in one session, time and energy permit only one exercise per body part. For example, you can only do one exercise for the upper back and one for the chest. When you do only one exercise per body part, it means that you can't train the muscles from as many angles as you'd like, to use bodybuilding terminology. Some muscle fibers, of necessity, are neglected.

In this routine, we solve that problem by doing two completely different weight workouts during the week. Including two separate whole-body workouts allows us to train each body part more completely.

But wait a minute, you may be thinking, that won't work because the B workout is easy. (That's the hard-day/easy-day system, of course.) So the muscles trained in the B workout aren't subjected to the same intensity. No problem! In the second week, we simply switch A and B. The B workout is done on Day One, so it becomes the hard session. The A workout becomes the second, or easy, session in the second week.

We include two different aerobic workouts for basically the same reason. As you'll remember, aerobic exercise conditions the muscles as well as the heart and lungs. It's only the involved muscles that benefit, however. To achieve total fitness, it's necessary to train the whole body (arms and legs) aerobically. This routine includes the treadmill for the lower body, and the Schwinn Air-Dyne, a stationary bicycle with push-pull arm action, for the upper body as well as the legs.

The treadmill is the hard workout, and the Air-Dyne session is done with less intensity. This, of course, shortchanges the upper body muscles. But rather than flip-flop the intensity week to week as we did with the weight workouts, we solve that problem differently this time. While the treadmill receives the main stress *throughout this routine,* and the Air-Dyne is always the easy session, in the second routine the emphasis is on the Air-Dyne; it becomes the hard workout.

In the third and last routine, the problem created by the hard-day/easy-day approach is solved in still another way, as you will see later. Some practical considerations dictate different solutions in each routine. Mainly, however, I want to show you that many variations of these routines are possible. I hope that will encourage you to be creative, later on, when formulating your own routines.

Many variations of these routines are possible—be creative when formulating your own routines.

The endurance phase starts in the first week. We begin with the endurance phase because it's the general conditioning phase. The light-poundage, high-repetition weight sessions and the relatively long and slow aerobic sessions prepare you physiologically for the low-volume, high-intensity workouts in the later phases.

Here's a summary of the entire 12-week training cycle in the A-B, Whole-Body Balanced Routine:

THE ENDURANCE PHASE
Weights — 20 Repetitions; Aerobics — 10 Min. Intervals

Week One

Day One:	Weight Workout A — 90%
Day Two:	Treadmill — Comfortable
Day Three:	Walk
Day Four:	Weight Workout B — 80%
Day Five:	Air-Dyne — Easy
Day Six:	Walk
Day Seven:	Rest

Week Two

Day One:	Weight Workout B — 90%
Day Two:	Treadmill — Comfortable
Day Three:	Walk
Day Four:	Weight Workout A — 80%
Day Five:	Air-Dyne — Easy
Day Six:	Walk
Day Seven:	Rest

Week Three

Day One:	Weight Workout A — 95%
Day Two:	Treadmill — Somewhat Hard
Day Three:	Walk
Day Four:	Weight Workout B — 85%
Day Five:	Air-Dyne — Comfortable
Day Six:	Walk
Day Seven:	Rest

Week Four

Day One:	Weight Workout B — 95%
Day Two:	Treadmill — Somewhat Hard
Day Three:	Walk
Day Four:	Weight Workout A — 85%
Day Five:	Air-Dyne — Comfortable
Day Six:	Walk
Day Seven:	Rest

THE STRENGTH AND ENDURANCE PHASE
Weights — 12 Repetitions; Aerobics — 5 Min. Intervals

Week Five

Day One:	Weight Workout A — 95%
Day Two:	Treadmill — Comfortable
Day Three:	Walk
Day Four:	Weight Workout B — 85%
Day Five:	Air-Dyne — Easy
Day Six:	Walk
Day Seven:	Rest

Week Six

Day One:	Weight Workout B — 95%
Day Two:	Treadmill — Somewhat Hard
Day Three:	Walk
Day Four:	Weight Workout A — 85%
Day Five:	Air-Dyne — Easy
Day Six:	Walk
Day Seven:	Rest

Week Seven

Day One:	Weight Workout A — 100%
Day Two:	Treadmill — Hard
Day Three:	Walk
Day Four:	Weight Workout B — 90%
Day Five:	Air-Dyne — Comfortable
Day Six:	Walk
Day Seven:	Rest

Week Eight

Day One:	Weight Workout B — 100%
Day Two:	Treadmill — Very Hard
Day Three:	Walk
Day Four:	Weight Workout A — 90%
Day Five:	Air-Dyne — Comfortable
Day Six:	Walk
Day Seven:	Rest

THE STRENGTH PHASE
Weights — 8 Repetitions; Aerobics — 1-2 Min. Intervals

Week Nine

Day One:	Weight Workout A — 100%
Day Two:	Treadmill — Comfortable
Day Three:	Walk
Day Four:	Weight Workout B — 90%
Day Five:	Air-Dyne — Easy
Day Six:	Walk
Day Seven:	Rest

Week 10

Day One:	Weight Workout B — 100%
Day Two:	Treadmill — Somewhat Hard
Day Three:	Walk
Day Four:	Weight Workout A — 90%
Day Five:	Air-Dyne — Easy
Day Six:	Walk
Day Seven:	Rest

Week 11

Day One:	Weight Workout A — 105%
Day Two:	Treadmill — Hard
Day Three:	Walk
Day Four:	Weight Workout B — 95%
Day Five:	Air-Dyne — Comfortable
Day Six:	Walk
Day Seven:	Rest

Week 12

Day One:	Weight Workout B — 105%
Day Two:	Treadmill — Very Hard
Day Three:	Walk
Day Four:	Weight Workout A — 95%
Day Five:	Air-Dyne — Comfortable
Day Six:	Walk
Day Seven:	Rest

Okay, now that you have an overview of this 12-week training cycle, let's look at Week One in detail.

WEEK ONE

THE ENDURANCE PHASE

Day One: Weight Workout A — 20 Repetitions — 90%
Brief General Warm-Up: Arm Curl and Extension, Shoulder Shrug, Arm Swing (forward and backward), Knee Lift, Toe Touch, Supported Knee Bend and Free Squat.

Barbell Squat:	warm-up and one work set
Leg Curl:	,,
Calf Raise on Leg Press:	,,
Behind-Neck Lat Pulldown:	,,
Barbell Bench Press:	,,
Seated Dumbbell Press:	,,
Triceps Cable Pushdown:	,,
Barbell Curl:	,,
Bent-Knee Sit-Up on Incline Board:	,,
(Hold weight on chest, if necessary, for added resistance.)	
One-Arm Dumbbell Side Bend:	,,
Brief General Cool-Down:	Same as General Warm-Up

In this workout, each work set consists of 20 repetitions. The intensity level is 90%. The percentage figure refers to your 20-

repetition maximum. In other words, if you are capable of 20 repetitions in the Barbell Squat with 200 pounds, then this workout calls for you to do 20 repetitions with 180 pounds.

Don't be confused. Despite the fact that this is the "hard day," you still use only 90% of your maximum weight for 20 repetitions. We usually start a phase with a weight that is comfortable. Not a light weight, mind you, but a poundage that's well within your capacity. We want to leave room for improvement in the later weeks of the phase. When in doubt, it's better to start a little lighter than you think you should. That way you can make progress throughout the phase. You approach or exceed your limit only at the end of the phase — and then you move on to the next phase.

When in doubt, it's better to start a little lighter than you think you should. That way you make progress throughout the phase.

This is a crucial part of the periodization system. You never face the encore problem discussed in Chapter Five, because you start well within yourself. You always know you can top yourself, lift more in the next workout. In other words, you set yourself up for a positive training experience. That keeps you coming back to the gym.

I do a brief general warm-up before starting my weight workout — nothing fancy, just enough to get the blood flowing and warm up the joints. I do 10 repetitions or so in each of the following movements: curl and extend the arms (rotate palms, up at the top and down on extension) to warm up the elbows; shrug the shoulders for the trapezius and upper back; swing the arms to the front and to the back (like swimming) for the shoulders; lift the knees alternately (like climbing bleachers) to loosen the hips; bend down and touch the toes (with knees bent) to warm up the lower back and hamstrings; and, finally, do some knee bends for the knees (the first few knee bends should be done with hands on floor to take some of the weight off the knees, then come upright and continue).

I recommend that you do this little routine or something similar at the start of all training sessions (weight and aerobics). It only takes a few minutes and it really helps you get in the mood to exercise.

I repeat the same movements at the end of each workout. This brings my circulation back to normal. It also helps my muscles get rid of waste products, which speeds recovery and reduces stiffness. Again, I recommend that you do the same.

A specific warm-up is also necessary for each weight exercise, especially when you only do one work set. With only one crack at it, you must be prepared to do your best on each exercise. That's

The Free Squat is one of the general warm-up movements that I do
without weights before and after each training session (weights
and aerobics). *Photo by Guy Appelman.*

what warm-up sets are for — they prepare your muscles and joints
for a maximum effort.

There's no set formula for warming up. The key is to do enough
to prepare for the work set — without wearing yourself out.

On exercises such as the Squat, where large muscles and heavy
weights are involved, more warm-up sets are required than on an
exercise such as the Curl, where small muscles and relatively light
weights are used. For example, I generally do two or three warm-
up sets on the Squat, two on the Bench Press, and only one warm-
up set for arm exercises.

There's no need to do the full number of repetitions on each
warm-up set, however. For example, if you plan to do 20 repetitions
with 200 pounds in the Squat, you might begin with 10 or 12 repetitions with 135 pounds, follow with eight at 175, and then two or
three reps with 190. Later, in the strength-endurance phase, as
well as the strength phase, where fewer repetitions and heavier
weights are called for, you might even want to add a warm-up
repetition or two with the weight you'll be using in the work set; I
find that this usually makes the hard set (i.e., the work set) go
better. It gives me the feel of the weight and bolsters my confi-

dence. Again, there's no fixed formula for warming up. After you've been at it for a while, your body will tell you how much warm-up is required.

You may also be wondering how much rest time to take between sets and exercises. Again, there's no rule, no set time. The best guide I can give you is this: don't rush, but don't let your muscles get cold, either. Simply rest long enough to catch your breath and prepare mentally for the next set. It stands to reason, of course, that you'll need more rest on an exhausting exercise like the Squat than on exercises such as the Triceps Pushdown, which causes little overall body fatigue. Take the rest you need, but don't sit around and lose your concentration or training drive; don't break the rhythm of your workout.

Some explanation of exercise form is also in order. The main thing to remember is *lift* the weight, don't fling it up. Move the weight with muscle, not momentum. Remember the all-or-none principle of muscle contraction discussed earlier? Your objective is to trigger as many muscle fibers as possible. That means you should do full-range, controlled repetitions. Try to get the most out of each repetition. Control the weight, feel it, while lifting and lowering.

Form is especially important on the Squat and Deadlift. These two movements are appropriately called multiple-muscle exercises because they involve many joints and muscles. The Squat and Deadlift are probably the most effective weight training exercises you can do; they stimulate the whole body to grow stronger. But they must be done with safety in mind.

The proper position in these two exercises is shown in the photographs (see page 158). On the Squat, don't round your back, and never go down fast and bounce out of the bottom position. If you have a tendency to lean forward and bend your back, place a small wedge under your heels for balance. On the Deadlift, the same guidelines apply: don't jerk, pull with your legs and keep your back straight as you come erect with the weight. The rule on these two exercises is ABC: Always Be Careful. (If you have a bad back or bad knees, consult your physician before doing Squats or Deadlifts.)

The order in which exercises are done is important. As you study this routine, you'll see that exercises for big muscle groups come first. That's because these exercises are the hardest; they require the most effort. Large body parts should be trained first, while you're still fresh.

Small muscles should be trained last — for two reasons. First, they don't require as much energy. Second, if the small muscles are trained first and become tired, they will interfere with the per-

The Barbell Squat, shown above, and the Deadlift, shown below, are probably the most effective weight training exercises you can do; they stimulate the whole body to grow stronger. But they must be done with safety in mind. Proper position is especially important on these two exercises, because you can work up to very heavy weights. The main thing to remember is to hold your back straight in both movements. On the Squat, don't allow your back to round and never go down fast or bounce out of the bottom position. On the Deadlift, don't attempt to jerk the weight off the floor; pull with the legs, slowly and smoothly, and keep your back straight as you come erect with the weight. Control the weight at all times, while lifting *and* lowering, on both exercises. Finally, if you have a bad back or bad knees, consult your physician before doing either movement. *Photos by Guy Appelman.*

formance of other exercises; they become a weak link, so to speak. For example, the triceps are involved in the Bench Press and the biceps are used in the Lat Pulldown. When these small muscles are fatigued, the large muscles of the chest and back can't be trained properly. In short, you can't do a good job on multiple-muscle exercises when some of the involved muscles are already tired.

In general, body parts should be trained in the following order: legs and lower back, quadriceps and hamstrings, calves, upper back, chest, shoulders, triceps, biceps and finally the waistline muscles (upper and lower abdominals, and obliques).

We do not have the time or space here to explain how to perform basic exercises. If you need further instruction in this area, please refer to the books listed in the "Help for Beginners" section.

Now let's move on to Day Two and the first aerobics session.

DAY TWO
Treadmill — Comfortable
Brief General Warm-Up: Same as Day One Weight Session.

Time	Speed	Grade	Effort
1 Minute	3.30 mph	0 Percent	Warm-Up
1	"	1	"
1	"	3	"
1	"	5	"
1	"	7	"
1	"	9	"
1	"	11	"
1	"	13	"
10	"	15	Work Period
5	"	10	Relief Interval
1	"	12.5	Transition
2	"	15	Work Period
2	3.50 mph	13	" "
2	3.70	11	" "
2	3.90	9	" "
2	4.10	7	" (jogging speed)
1	3.30	7	Cool-Down
1	"	5	"
1	"	3	"
1	"	1	"
2	"	0	"

40 minutes total
5-10 minutes: Brief General Cool-Down (Same as Warm-Up) and Stretch

This, of course, is an aerobic workout. It will strengthen your heart-lung system. What's more, it will increase the fat-burning capacity of the muscles in your lower body.

In my training, the overall intensity level in this workout is "comfortable." Not hard or easy but, as was the case in the weight workout on Day One, a level that allows me to progress as the endurance phase unfolds. Now your task is to adjust treadmill speed or grade to an intensity that's comfortable for you as well. This may take some experimentation, but you'll soon find the correct settings. At the start, it's probably a good idea to use less speed or grade whenever you are in doubt. There's always time to increase intensity later.

I prefer the treadmill to outdoor workouts because of the control it gives me. On the treadmill, speed or incline is easy to adjust. I can create hills as gentle or steep as I like — with a touch of my fingertips. And there's never any dogs or traffic.

Those who say treadmills are boring haven't tried a workout like this. Look at the variety!

Equally important, the treadmill is easier on my joints than the pavement or a track. That's because I can make it more difficult by increasing the angle of incline without upping the speed! That means I can work hard — very hard — and still walk. There's no need to jar my joints by jogging or running. Again, it's like a hill I can adjust at will. As anyone who has ever hiked up a steep grade knows only too well, you *can* get a good workout without running.

Those who say treadmills are boring haven't tried a workout like this. Look at the variety! The speed or grade changes constantly. In the first eight minutes (the warm-up period), the grade increases every minute. The first 10-minute work period comes at a 15% grade. For me, that's a comfortable angle, but still challenging. After that, the incline drops to 10% for a five-minute relief interval, which gives you a welcome break. The next minute at 12.5% grade serves as a transition into the next work period. (I never increase the incline precipitously. Elevating the tread gradually, in stages, helps to avoid overstretching the calf muscles.)

I mentioned earlier that I don't like doing the same exercise twice. That goes for treadmill workouts as well. As you can see, the second 10-minute work period is different; the speed increases and the grade decreases every two minutes. The last two minutes, at 4.10 mph, is actually too fast for walking, so you have to break into a jog. Believe me, the changes keep you busy — and challenged. There's no time to get bored. The workout ends with a six-minute gradual cool-down.

On the treadmill, you can work hard — very hard — and still walk;
you simply make it more difficult by increasing the angle of
incline, without upping the speed. That's much easier on the joints
than running. *Photo by Guy Appelman.*

Carol and I have our treadmill set up in front of the TV. She likes to watch old movies, and I usually watch the news on CNN. This adds further interest and variety to the treadmill session. Along with the changes in speed and grade, the television makes our workouts fly by.

As I'm sure you know, motorized treadmills are expensive. Nevertheless, Carol and I consider the money we paid for ours well spent. We love our treadmill (purchased from Pacer Industries in Dallas, Tex.). If you can't see your way clear to purchasing a treadmill, you'll find them in most well-equipped fitness centers. But if you can't buy a treadmill and don't have access to one, this workout can be done outdoors.

All you need is a good pair of running shoes and a watch. Walk, jog or run at a comfortable pace — not too hard or easy — during the first 10-minute work period. Slow down for five minutes, and then pick up the speed for another 10 minutes. On the second work period, vary your pace to make it more interesting. And if there's a hill in your neighborhood, by all means put it to use.

Whatever alternative you choose, be sure to spend a few minutes warming up and cooling down. Stretching at the end of the workout, while your muscles are still warm and pliant, is a good idea as well.

The best time to stretch is after your workout, not before; because that's when your muscles are warm and pliant. Stretching is *not* a good way to warm up. Stretching should be done *only* after you are warmed up. *Photo by Guy Appelman.*

DAY THREE
Walk

After two conscientious workouts, you deserve a rest — at least a partial rest. As mentioned earlier, I usually walk about 30 minutes after lunch and another 30 minutes in the evening. That's what I recommend you do on Day Three.

I even walk on days when I lift weights or do aerobics. This burns a few extra calories, of course, but it serves another purpose as well. I've found that walking does more to speed recovery than complete rest. Walking increases your circulation, which facilitates the flow of nutrients to all parts of the body; it also helps your muscles unload waste products.

What I really like best about walking, however, is that it makes me feel good, physically and emotionally. I feel refreshed and renewed after I walk.

Keep one thing in mind, however, on Day Three: you're walking to speed recovery. This is active rest, not a race. Just stroll along at a pleasant pace. Stop to smell the flowers. Enjoy yourself! That's what I do.

DAY FOUR
Weight Workout B — 20 repetitions — 80%

Brief General Warm-Up:	Same As Day One
Deadlift:	warm-up and one work set
Leg Extension:	"
Standing Calf Raise:	"
Bent-Over Two-Arm Dumbbell Row:	"
Parallel Bar Dip:	"
Behind-Neck Press:	"
Narrow-Grip Bench Press (for triceps):	"
Preacher-Bench Barbell Curl:	"
Hip Curl (see photos next page):	"
Twisting Sit-Up On Incline Board:	"
Brief General Cool-Down:	Same as General Warm-Up

This is the other whole-body weight workout in this routine. It stresses all the major muscle groups, but from different angles than the exercises in Weight Workout A. For example, the Deadlift is substituted for the Squat. Both exercises work the thighs, hips and lower back, but in a different manner. The Deadlift places the stress on the lower back, while the Squat puts more emphasis on the thighs. The most complete development results when you do both.

The Hip Curl is my favorite exercise for the lower abdominal muscles. The starting position is shown in the upper photo and the finishing position is shown below. Start with your hips almost touching the incline board, and keeping the tension on your lower abs, curl your hips up towards your rib cage. If you feel the tension go off the lower abs, you have lowered or raised your hips too much. Change the resistance by varying the angle of the board or adding ankle weights. Do this exercise correctly, and you'll really feel the action in your lower abdominal muscles. *Photos by Mike Neveux.*

To further illustrate this point, the Bent-Over Dumbbell Row, included here, works the lower lats, while the Behind-Neck Pull-down, included in the A Workout, stresses the lats further up. The Bench Press, included in Workout A, affects the center of the pectoral muscles and the Parallel Bar Dip, in this B session, works the lower and outer part of the chest. When you do the exercises, the points of stress are obvious. You can feel the difference.

The variety in the two weight workouts, of course, makes training more fun. In this first week, Workout B is the easy session. But, as you know, in the second week B becomes the hard session and A is done with less intensity. The repetitions remain the same, however: 20 repetitions on work sets in both the hard and easy sessions.

The intensity in this workout is 80%. You'll find that makes the exercises pretty easy. For example, if you're capable of 20 repetitions in an exercise with 100 pounds, doing 80 pounds is a breeze. But that doesn't mean it's a waste of time.

As stated earlier, research has shown that it's best not to train a body part heavily more than once a week. It's a good idea, however, to train the muscle a second time each week with less intensity. The second workout, the easy session, prevents backsliding — muscle strength starts to decline after about five days — without depressing the immune system or overstressing the body in other ways. Thus, the lighter workout maintains strength without delaying recovery.

Research has shown that it's best not to train a bodypart heavy more than once a week.

Plus, some of my most enjoyable workouts come on easy days. With lighter weights, you don't have to focus so much on getting the weight up. You have more opportunity to feel the muscles working. You can concentrate on form, stretching the muscle at the beginning of each rep and lifting the weight slowly, through a full range of motion. Doing it this way, you learn how your muscles function. It's like examining an action in slow motion. And it feels great!

You may be tempted to use more than 80%, but don't do it. You'll get your chance to push yourself later. Believe me, the heavy days in this routine will come around soon enough.

Finally, with lighter weights, you won't need as many warm-up sets. Nevertheless, it's still a good idea to do a warm-up set or two, especially on multiple-muscle exercises such as the Deadlift.

The Two-Arm Dumbbell Rowing exercise included in this routine can also be done with one arm, as shown in these photos. Note the full range of motion, the stretch at the bottom of the movement and the full contraction at the top. That's what it takes to work a muscle fully. *Photos by Chris Lund.*

DAY FIVE
Air-Dyne — Easy

Brief General Warm-Up: Same as before

Time	Load	Effort
5 minutes	1-3	Warm-Up
10	3.50	Work Period
5	2.50	Relief Interval
2	3.50	Work Period
2	4.00	,,
2	3.00	,,
2	3.75	,,
2	3.25	,,
5	3-1	Cool-Down

30 minutes total

5-10 minutes: Brief General Cool-Down and Stretch

I'm often asked what is my favorite piece of aerobic exercise equipment. My answer is always the same: the Schwinn Air-Dyne. As you already know, the Air-Dyne is a stationary bicycle with push-pull arm action. It utilizes air resistance (air passes through wind vanes on the wheel) to provide synchronized work for the arms and legs. The faster the wheel is turned by the pedals and arm levers, the greater the air resistance and the amount of effort required.

The Air-Dyne is equipped with a work-load indicator which shows how fast/hard you're working. On bikes made prior to 1989, the indicator goes from .50 (very easy) up to 7.00 and above (very hard). Units made in 1989 and thereafter have a computerized performance monitor with a different load scale. On the newer models, respective work loads occur at lower speeds (RPMs). For example, a load reading of 3.00 comes at 50 RPM on the older model, whereas 50 RPM on the new monitor produces a load read-out of 5.00. In other words, on the newer Air-Dynes the effort at a given load is less.

The "load" figures given in this workout and those that follow are from the older monitor. The top load in this workout, 4.00, would be approximately 6.50 on the newer units. The precise ratio really isn't important. All you need to remember is that there's a difference in the old and new performance monitors. Otherwise, all Schwinn Air-Dynes are the same.

The Air-Dyne is reasonably priced and can be purchased at Schwinn bicycle shops. Carol and I bought ours in 1983 after it was called to our attention by psychologist Richard Winett, a good friend and lifetime weight trainer. He said it was much better than

The Schwinn Air-Dyne is my favorite piece of aerobic exercise equipment. The Air-Dyne provides aerobic exercise for the whole body. That's important, of course, because only the involved muscles benefit from aerobic exercise. Plus, you can exercise more and harder when you stress the legs *and* the arms. *Photo by Guy Appelman.*

a regular stationary bicycle. And he was right.

After almost a decade, the Air-Dyne is still the aerobic exercise machine I use most frequently. What's more, it seems that I'm not the only one who enjoys riding the Air-Dyne. Schwinn has had great success with the unit — so much so that other companies have come out with copycat models.

The main advantage of the Air-Dyne (and other similar machines) is that it provides aerobic exercise for the whole body. As already explained, in this routine the Air-Dyne is an excellent complement to the treadmill. Whereas the treadmill works the legs, with the Air-Dyne you can spread the fat-burning and conditioning benefits of aerobic exercise to the upper body as well.

When the stress of aerobic exercise is spread over a greater volume of muscle, you can exercise more and harder without running the risk of injury.

Moreover, with a combination of the treadmill and the Air-Dyne, your body can tolerate more aerobic exercise. The chances of developing overuse injuries would be greater if only the treadmill was used in this routine. When the stress of aerobic exercise is spread over a greater volume of muscle, as it is here by using both the treadmill and the Air-Dyne, you can exercise more and harder without running the risk of injury. It's a lot more fun as well.

The work loads indicated here are mine — as was the case in the treadmill workout. An important point, again, is that these load figures aren't indicated so that you can, or should, copy them. Rather, they are provided to illustrate how the effort varies in the course of this workout.

Your overall effort should be "easy." The load-indicator readings shown are easy... for me. For you, the same work load may be hard, moderate or very easy. So it's up to you to make the necessary adjustments.

I'll warn you now: the perceived effort increases later, especially when we emphasize the Air-Dyne in the next routine. Please allow plenty of room for improvement. Cut yourself some slack at this point. Choose a work load that is truly easy.

DAY SIX
Walk

Walk again — to accelerate your recovery. But go slow; enjoy yourself!

DAY SEVEN
Rest

Day Seven is rest day, but you don't have to rest completely — unless you want to. For me, this day falls on Sunday. Carol and I usually take a long walk in the foothills above our house. If you feel like doing something similar, go ahead.

Or maybe you just want to go to church in the morning and rest in the afternoon with your family. That's fine, too. Day Seven is a day for relaxation, a day to do whatever pleases you.

A Word to the Wise

A final note before we move on: if you follow my advice and keep the intensity relatively low during the first week, you'll be feeling good at this point. That's because this routine builds your morale as well as your body. Ask yourself, "Am I looking forward to Week Two?" If the answer is "yes," you're off to a good start.

> **An unusual pain during or after an exercise is a message from your body that something is wrong.**

If, on the other hand, the answer is "no," you probably started at an unsustainable pace. You were too aggressive, in other words. It's very important that you don't make that mistake. If you find yourself in this situation, go back and re-evaluate your first week. Cut back your poundages and your intensity levels on the aerobic workouts to a point that makes you want to continue.

Now you're ready to move on to Week Two.

WEEK TWO

Day One: Weight Workout B — 20 Repetitions — 90%

As explained earlier, this workout is the same one you did on Day Four of the first week. The only difference is the intensity. This week Weight Workout B is the hard weight session, whereas last week it was the easy session. You do it at 90% intensity this week. Again, that means 90% of your 20-repetition maximum. For example, if you are capable of 20 reps in the Deadlift with 150 pounds, use 135 in this workout.

Remember the ABC rule (Always Be Careful)? Another time-honored rule is: if it hurts, don't do it. An unusual pain during or after an exercise is a message from your body that something is wrong. If you experience pain (other than the normal discomfort of exercise), stop! And if the pain persists, consult your physician. Listen to your body.

DAY TWO
Treadmill — Comfortable

(Same as Week One)

Keep in mind that the endurance phase is a general conditioning period. It builds an endurance base to prepare you for the more
intense but shorter sessions coming up. At this point, you should
be in no hurry to increase treadmill speed. Take advantage of the
two weeks required to do both the A and B weight sessions at 90%
intensity. Repeat the "comfortable" treadmill session from last
week.

If you haven't used a treadmill before, you'll probably welcome
another chance to operate the grade and speed controls. Later,
when the sessions are harder, there won't be as much time to think
about which button to push. Believe me, simply keeping up with
the treadmill will require almost all your concentration.

What's more, if you've been doing steady-pace aerobic workouts
in the past, it may take some time to get used to the varying intensity level in each of these aerobic sessions. Once you get the hang of
it, however, you'll find the variety enjoyable. There's no time to
get bored.

DAY THREE
Walk

DAY FOUR
Weight Workout A — 20 Reps — 80%

(Same as Week One, but at 80% intensity.)

This week Weight Workout A is the easy session. Don't forget:
the intensity drops to 80% this time.

DAY FIVE
Air-Dyne — Easy

(Same as Week One)

DAY SIX
Walk

DAY SEVEN
Rest

WEEK THREE

Day One: Weight Workout A — 20 Reps — 95%

As promised, the effort gets harder as the phase progresses. Here, in the third week of the endurance phase, we increase the intensity to 95%. That's "somewhat hard." For example, if your 20-rep maximum in the Squat is 200 pounds, you have to work pretty hard to do 95% of that, which is 20 reps with 190. Still, you know you're good for more. That's the way it should be at this point. You still have plenty of enthusiasm and reserve to complete this phase, and then move on to the strength and endurance phase later.

So hold back a little here. Save your best effort for later, when the suggested intensity level will be "hard." If in doubt, use less weight, rather than more.

DAY TWO
Treadmill — Somewhat Hard

Brief General Warm-Up: Same as before

Time	Speed	Grade	Effort
1 Minute	3.30 MPH	1 percent	Warm-Up
1	"	3	"
1	3.50	"	"
1	"	5	"
1	"	7	"
1	"	9	"
1	"	11	"
1	"	13	"
10	"	15	Work Period
4	3.30	10	Relief Interval
1	3.50	"	Transition
1	"	12.5	"
2	"	15	Work Period
2	3.70	13	"
2	3.90	11	"
2	4.10	9 (Jog)	"
2	4.30	7 (Jog)	"
1	3.30	7	Cool-Down
1	"	5	"
1	"	3	"
1	"	1	"
2	2.80	0	"

40 minutes total

5-10 minutes: Brief General Cool-Down and Stretch

I upped the ante here, just as I did in the last weight workout. The major difference between this treadmill workout and the previous two is the speed. In the third minute, you'll notice, speed increases to 3.50 mph. It remains at 3.50 as the grade increases, gradually, to 15% for the 10-minute work period.

In the second work period, the speed starts higher than before (3.50 vs. 3.30) and, therefore, ends up higher, at 4.30. As a result, the jog period doubles — to two minutes.

The underlying principle of training: As the stress is gradually increased, the body is forced to adapt and become stronger.

The overall speed increase, 0.20 miles per hour or about 6%, may not seem like much, but it's a substantial increase. For me, it elevates the intensity of this workout from "comfortable" to "somewhat hard." As always, your task is to adjust the speed and grade, up or down, to make the intensity somewhat hard for your level of fitness.

DAY THREE
Walk

DAY FOUR
Weight Workout B — 20 reps — 85%

As you can see, the intensity level on the easy day increases as well. On Day One of this week, the intensity of the hard weight session increased 5% to 95%. Likewise, the intensity in this easy session increases from 80 to 85%.

As mentioned several times before, the overall intensity increases as we move through each phase. That's the underlying principle of training: as the stress is gradually increased, the body is forced to adapt and become stronger. Little by little, we'll continue to do that as we move through each phase.

DAY FIVE
Air-Dyne — Comfortable

Brief General Warm-Up: Same as before

Time	Load	Effort
2 minutes	2.00	Warm-Up
3	3.00	”
10	4.00	Work Period
5	3.00	Relief Interval
2	4.00	Work Period
2	3.50	”
2	4.50	”

173

Day Five (cont.)

2	3.75	Work Period
2	4.25	"
5	3-1	Cool-Down

35 minutes total

5-10 minutes: Brief General Cool-Down and Stretch

The intensity, of course, increases here as well. In the first two weeks, the basic load level (excluding warm-up and cool-down) was 3.50. In this workout the load increases to 4.00.

When I ride an Air-Dyne, a load of 4.00 is "comfortable" for me. You'll need to experiment to find the load level that you perceive as comfortable.

As indicated earlier, all the Air-Dyne workouts can be done on a pedals-only stationary bike or a regular (outdoor) bicycle. Simply vary the load or speed as indicated.

You'll recall from our earlier discussion of cross-training that pedaling a bicycle stresses different muscles than running (outdoors or on a treadmill). That's why Frank Shorter does both; it allows him to train more and harder without breaking down.

DAY SIX
Walk

DAY SEVEN
Rest

WEEK FOUR

Day One: Weight Workout B — 20 repetitions — 95%

Last week we did Weight Workout A at 95% intensity. This week Weight Workout B becomes the hard session, so it's done at 95% intensity.

DAY TWO
Treadmill — Somewhat Hard

(Same as Week Three)

DAY THREE
Walk

DAY FOUR
Weight Workout A — 20 repetitions — 85%

DAY FIVE
Air-Dyne — Comfortable

(Same as Week Three)

DAY SIX
Walk

DAY SEVEN
Rest

That's the end of the endurance phase. You're now ready to move on to the next phase.

WEEK FIVE
THE STRENGTH AND ENDURANCE PHASE
Day One: Weight Workout A — 12 Reps — 95%

The main change in this new phase is the intensity: the poundages go up, and the repetitions go down. The effect is dramatic. Twelve reps place a different stress on the muscles than 20 reps. The change is readily apparent. You can feel it.

As explained in Chapter Five, the high repetitions used in the endurance phase stress the endurance components of the muscle cell (the mitochondria), while low repetitions stress the contractile or strength components (the myofibrils). The 12 repetitions we'll be doing here fall in the mid-range, of course, and stress both the strength and endurance components of the muscle. As noted earlier, it takes a full range of repetitions to fully develop a muscle.

When you do 20 repetitions, as was the case in the previous phase, you feel a burn or pump in your muscles. That means the mitochondria are getting a good workout. The pump and burn are caused by the accumulation of lactic acid. The number of repetitions you can do before lactic acid buildup shuts down the muscle is largely determined by the capacity of the mitochondria to utilize oxygen. That's because oxygen allows lactic acid to be broken down to produce energy for further contractions.

On the other hand, when you use a heavier weight that only permits eight repetitions, there isn't sufficient pump (or buildup of lactic acid) to terminate the set, so the contractile strength of the myofibrils is the limiting factor. As mentioned earlier, the mid-range repetitions used here stress both the mitochondria and the myofibrils.

Knowing what you're trying to accomplish in each phase allows you to maximize the effect by changing the way you lift. During the endurance phase it's advisable to do slow, continuous reps to work the mitochondria. In other words, go for the burn. In the final phase, the strength phase, which stresses the myofibrils, I suggest you lift faster and pause briefly between reps to let the pump subside. When you follow this approach, lactic acid doesn't interfere and the muscle can contract to its limit. Here, in the strength-and-endurance phase, take a mid-course. Perform each lift with moderate speed and pause momentarily between reps. Altering the speed of the exercise in this way emphasizes the change from phase to phase and makes training more productive — and interesting. Again, you can really feel the difference.

Knowing what you're trying to accomplish in each phase allows you to maximize the effect by changing the way you lift. Altering the speed of the exercise as described in the text emphasizes the change from phase to phase and makes training more productive — and interesting. *Photo by Guy Appelman.*

Obviously, you'll be able to use more weight in this phase than you did in the endurance phase. If you can do 20 reps in an exercise with 100 pounds, then you can probably use 115 or 120 when you only do 12 reps. If you don't already know your 12-rep maximum on an exercise, you'll have to find out by experimentation. As always, when in doubt use less weight.

Keep in mind that the intensity in this workout is 95%. That means you'll use a little less than maximum weight. The practical effect will be that you stop each exercise about one repetition short of your limit. When you hit 12, you'll be good for one more rep, but don't do it! We'll pick up the slack in Weeks Seven and Eight where the intensity increases to 100%. So, again, save a little bit for later.

When heavier weights are used, warm-up becomes more critical. A cold muscle simply can't perform up to it's capacity.

Finally, when heavier weights are used, as they are here, warm-up becomes more critical. A cold muscle simply can't perform up to its capacity. Be sure to do two or three warm-up sets before tackling your work set. As mentioned earlier, you might want to do a final warm-up set of two or three repetitions with the weight you'll be using in the work set. I find that this gives me confidence and makes the work set go better.

DAY TWO
Treadmill — Comfortable

Brief General Warm-Up: Same as before

Time	Speed	Grade	Effort
1 Minute	3.30 mph	0 Percent	Warm-Up
1	"	2	"
1	"	4	"
1	"	6	"
1	"	8	"
1	"	10	"
1	"	12	"
1	"	14	"
1	"	16	"
1	"	18	"
5	"	20	Work Period
4	"	10	Relief Interval
1	"	14	Transition
1	"	17	"
1	"	20	Work Period
1	3.50	18	"

Day Two (cont.)

1	3.70	16	Work Period
1	3.90	14	"
1	4.10	12 (Jog)	"
5	3.30	10	Relief Interval
1	3.70	"	Work Period
1	3.90	"	"
1	4.10	" (Jog)	"
1	4.30	" (Jog)	"
1	4.50	" (Jog)	"
1	3.30	"	Cool-Down
1	"	5	"
1	2.80	"	"
1	"	0	"

40 minutes total

5-10 minutes: Brief General Cool-Down and Stretch

The treadmill workouts in this phase are different as well. As was the case in the last weight session, the volume decreases and the intensity increases. The treadmill work periods in the endurance phase ran 10 minutes. Here the work periods are cut to five minutes, and the grade is increased from 15 to 20%. In addition, the relief intervals are proportionally longer to compensate for the greater intensity.

In effect, we switch from a long, gradually sloping hill to one that is shorter and steeper. For every five minutes climbing the hill, we take a break of equal length. You'll recall, of course, that in the endurance phase the work/relief ratio was 2 to 1, 10 minutes work and five minutes relief.

Again, this treadmill workout has plenty of variety. There are three work periods, all different. Even so, the changes follow a logical pattern; they're easy to remember.

The first 10 minutes constitute a gradual warm-up period; the grade increases every minute, in small jumps, from 0 to 18%. As in previous treadmill workouts, the first work period is done at a constant speed and grade, 3.30 mph and 20%. Then comes a welcome four-minute break, followed by two minutes of transition. The second work period is different. This time the speed increases and the grade decreases every minute. That's followed by another five minutes of relief. The last work period is another variation. The speed increases every minute, as in the second work period, but this time the grade stays at 10%.

As the speed increases on a treadmill, there eventually comes a point where it's easier to jog than walk. That happens in this workout as it did in the earlier sessions. In the second work period,

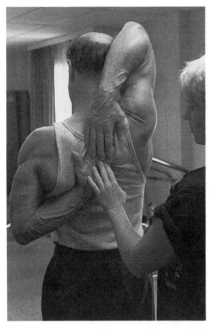

The complete medical and physical evaluation at The Cooper Clinic includes a test of your flexibility. My upper body flexibility level was graded "very good" and my lower back-hamstring flexibility was found to be "excellent." I attribute my favorable flexibility scores to years of lifting weights through a full range of motion. Recently I have also added stretching to my training program (twice a week, after aerobic exercise sessions). That probably contributed to my flexibility scores as well. *Photos by Justin Joseph.*

there is one minute of jogging. In the last work period, treadmill speed dictates three minutes of jogging.

Again, there's no time to get bored. From the first minute onward, you'll be busy and challenged.

As always, this workout should be adjusted to suit your level of fitness. The speeds and grades shown are mine. Adjust them so this workout is "comfortable" for you. Again, when in doubt use a slower speed or gentler grade. That's important because we'll up the ante each week. This workout becomes "somewhat hard," "hard" and, finally, "very hard."

Whatever you do, don't skip the four minutes of cool-down at the end. This helps to bring your heart rate and circulation back to normal. To finish the job, follow that with 5-10 minutes of general cool-down and stretching. (The time to stretch is after — not before — a workout because that's when your muscles are warm and pliant.)

Again, remember to hold back in this first week. You'll need some reserve capacity for the harder workouts to follow.

DAY THREE
Walk

DAY FOUR
Weight Workout B — 12 Reps — 85%

On Day Four switch to the B weight workout. Do 12 repetitions. The intensity level is 85%, so this time stop each work set about two reps short of your limit. Remember, this workout is the easy session. And don't forget to warm up.

DAY FIVE
Air-Dyne — Easy

Brief General Warm-Up: Same as before

Time	Load	Effort
1 minutes	2.00	Warm-Up
2	3.00	,,
2	3.75	,,
5	4.50	Work Period
5	3.00	Relief Interval
1	4.50	Work Period
1	4.00	,,
1	5.00	,,
1	4.25	,,
1	4.75	,,

Day Five (cont.)

5	4-2	Cool-Down

25 minutes total

5-10 minutes: Brief General Cool-Down and Stretch

As in the Day Two treadmill workout, the work periods here are shortened to five minutes. Also, the work load increases from 4.00 in the last Air-Dyne workout of the endurance phase to 4.50 here.

Remember, this is the easy aerobic session. Adjust the load as necessary to make this session "easy." Again, the load figures shown are for illustration only. They're what I use on my pre-1989-model Air-Dyne. If you have a late-model Air-Dyne, your load figures will probably be higher.

DAY SIX
Walk

DAY SEVEN
Rest

WEEK SIX

Day One: Weight Workout B — 12 Reps — 95%

Following the same pattern used in the endurance phase, the B Weight Workout becomes the hard session in the second week. Do 12 repetitions in each work set at 95% intensity. Again, this means that the 12th repetition should be a little short of your limit.

DAY TWO
Treadmill — Somewhat Hard

Brief General Warm-Up: Same as before

Time	Speed	Grade	Effort
1 Minute	3.30 mph	0 Percent	Warm-Up
1	"	2	"
1	"	4	"
1	"	6	"
1	"	8	"
1	3.50	10	"
1	"	12	"
1	"	14	"
1	"	16	"
1	"	18	"
5	"	20	Work Period
4	3.30	10	Relief Interval

Day Two (cont.)

1	3.30	15	Transition
1	3.50	”	”
1	”	20	Work Period
1	3.70	18	”
1	3.90	16	”
1	4.10	14 (Jog)	”
1	4.30	12 (Jog)	”
5	3.30	10	Relief Interval
1	3.90	”	Work Period
1	4.10	” (Jog)	”
1	4.30	” (Jog)	”
1	4.50	” (Jog)	”
1	4.70	” (Jog)	”
1	3.00	”	Cool-Down
1	”	5	”
1	2.50	”	”
1	”	0	”

40 minutes total

5-10 minutes: Brief General Cool-Down and Stretch

As promised, this treadmill workout is harder than the last one. The main difference is that the speed is increased to 3.50 miles per hour. You'll recall that's the same increase we made in Week Three of the endurance phase. It doesn't seem like much but, as you know, it makes a substantial difference. It upgrades this workout from "comfortable" to "somewhat hard."

If you find that you overestimated your ability by starting too high in Week Five, don't hesitate to make a mid-course correction at this point. Set the speed and grade so that you're sure you'll be able to increase the intensity next week and again in Week Eight.

DAY THREE
Walk

DAY FOUR
Weight Workout A — 12 Reps — 85%

Since Weight Workout A becomes the lighter workout this week, do it with a little less weight than you used in Week Five.

DAY FIVE
Air-Dyne — Easy

(Same as Week Five)

DAY SIX
Walk

DAY SEVEN
Rest

WEEK SEVEN

Day One: Weight Workout A — 12 Reps — 100%

Remember that rep you saved or kept in reserve last week? Do it this week. Make the 12th rep in each work set your limit.

Please don't cheat (i.e., abandon proper form) to make the last rep, however. You should be able to do all 12 repetitions in good form; hold your position and don't jerk or throw the weight. If you can't do 12 reps with strict form, use less weight.

This workout should be hard, but not so hard that it saps your enthusiasm. Lifting weights should be a rewarding experience — hard, but satisfying. Select poundages that provide you with a sense of accomplishment *and* make you want to return to the gym!

DAY TWO
Treadmill — Hard

Brief General Warm-Up: Same as before

Time	Speed	Grade	Effort
1 Minute	3.30 mph	1 Percent	Warm-up
1	,,	2	,,
1	,,	4	,,
1	,,	6	,,
1	,,	8	,,
1	3.50	10	,,
1	,,	12	,,
1	,,	14	,,
1	3.70	16	,,
1	,,	18	,,
5	,,	20	Work Period
4	3.30	10	Relief Interval
1	3.50	15	Transition
1	3.70	,,	,,
1	,,	20	Work Period
1	3.90	18	,,
1	4.10	16 (Jog)	,,
1	4.30	14 (Jog)	,,
1	4.50	12 (Jog)	,,

Day Two (cont.)

5	3.30	10	Relief Interval
1	4.10	" (Jog)	Work Period
1	4.30	" (Jog)	"
1	4.50	" (Jog)	"
1	4.70	" (Jog)	"
1	4.90	" (Jog)	"
1	3.00	"	Cool-Down
1	"	5	"
1	2.50	"	"
1	"	0	"

40 minutes total

5-10 minutes: Brief General Cool-Down and Stretch

Here the intensity increases again. The basic work-period speed increases to 3.70 miles per hour (from 3.50). In my training that makes this workout "hard." Not so hard, however, that I can't up the ante again in Week Eight. Make the necessary adjustments so you'll be able to do the same.

DAY THREE
Walk

DAY FOUR
Weight Workout B — 12 Reps — 90%

Use a little more weight than you did in the first week of this phase. But don't lose sight of the fact that this is the easy session. You should be able to do the 12th repetition on each work set comfortably.

DAY FIVE
Air-Dyne — Comfortable

Brief General Warm-Up: Same as before

Time	Load	Effort
1 Minute	2.00 mph	Warm-Up
2	3.00	"
2	4.00	"
5	5.00	Work Period
5	3.00	Relief Interval
1	5.00	Work Period
1	4.50	"
1	5.50	"
1	4.75	"

Day Five (cont.)

| 1 | 5.25 | Work Period |
| 5 | 4-2 | Cool-Down |

25 minutes total

5-10 minutes: Brief General Cool-Down and Stretch

This workout is a little harder than the Air-Dyne session in Week Six. Still, it should be "comfortable." Always remember that the second aerobic session in each week is the easy day.

DAY SIX
Walk

DAY SEVEN
Rest

Lifting weights should be a rewarding experience — hard, but satisfying. Select poundages that provide you with a sense of accomplishment and make you want to return to the gym! *Photo by Guy Appelman.*

WEEK EIGHT

Day One: Weight Workout B — 12 reps — 100%

This week push the B workout to the limit. The 12th rep in each work set should be hard. At the end of this session you should be able to say to yourself: "I did a good job. I worked hard. I'm proud of myself. I'm ready for the strength phase."

DAY TWO
Treadmill — Very Hard

Brief General Warm-Up: Same as before

Time	Speed	Grade	Effort
1 Minute	3.30 mph	0 Percent	Warm-Up
1	"	2	"
1	"	4	"
1	"	6	"
1	3.50	8	"
1	"	10	"
1	3.70	12	"
1	"	14	"
1	3.90	16	"
1	"	18	"
5	"	20	Work Period
4	3.30	10	Relief Interval
1	3.60	15	Transition
1	3.90	"	"
1	"	20	Work Period
1	4.10	18 (Jog)	"
1	4.30	16 (Jog)	"
1	4.50	14 (Jog)	"
1	4.70	12 (Jog)	"
5	3.30	10	Relief Interval
1	4.30	" (Jog)	Work Period
1	4.50	" (Jog)	"
1	4.70	" (Jog)	"
1	4.90	" (Jog)	"
1	5.10	" (Jog)	"
1	3.00	"	Cool-Down
1	"	5	"
1	2.50	"	"
1	"	0	"

40 minutes total

5-10 minutes: Brief General Cool-Down and Stretch

186

After this workout I wrote in my training diary: "Boy, that was tough! I'm glad I won't have to do that again for a while."

That's the beauty of periodization. After a really hard workout like this, you back off for a while. Then you gradually work up to another hard workout at the end of the next phase.

Exercise physiologists call this "overload" training. Overload makes you get better.

All-out sessions like this are important, however. They force your body to adapt and grow stronger. If you don't push to the limit from time to time, pretty soon your limit shrinks. It's the old story: use it or lose it.

If you want to improve, you must challenge your body. You must push it to the limit and beyond at times. Exercise physiologists call this "overload training." Overload is what makes you get better.

So get cranked up for this workout. Give it your best shot. Then pat yourself on the back — and take comfort in the fact that the next "very hard" treadmill session won't come until the end of the next phase.

DAY THREE
Walk

DAY FOUR
Weight Workout A — 12 Reps — 90%

DAY FIVE
Air-Dyne — Comfortable

(Same as Week Seven)

DAY SIX
Walk

DAY SEVEN
Rest

WEEK NINE

THE STRENGTH PHASE
Day One: Weight Workout A — 8 Reps — 100%

The primary goal of training, of course, is to improve on your previous best. Up to this point the weight workouts haven't called for you to exceed your previous limits. In the endurance phase, you started with 90% of your 20-rep maximum in the first week and moved up to 95% in Week Four. The strength and endurance phase started at 95% and ended with 100% of your 12-rep limit. To put it another way, in the first eight weeks you merely flirted with your personal records (PR's). Now, in the strength phase, you are ready to challenge yourself and go for new PR's.

That's why this phase starts at 100% intensity. In the first two weeks you equal your previous eight-rep maximums (in Weight Workout A the first week, Weight Workout B the second week). Think of those workouts as dress rehearsals. Then, in the final two weeks, pull out all the stops and go for 105%!

In other words, if your eight-rep best in an exercise is 100 pounds, you'll duplicate that in the first part of this phase, and then at the end of the phase, you'll do eight reps with 105 pounds. That's the beauty of phase training or periodization: the early phases prepare you physically and psychologically — they give you confidence — to exceed your previous best in the final phase. You might say that the "moment of truth" comes in this phase. But don't worry; with the first two phases under your belt, you're ready!

> **The beauty of phase training or periodization is the early phases prepare you physically and psychologically— and give you the confidence to exceed your previous best.**

If you don't know your eight-rep maximum in an exercise, you'll have to experiment again. As a rule of thumb, a drop in reps from 12 to eight allows most people to increase the weight by about 10%. So, in the first two weeks, you might add 10% to the weights used at the end of the 12-rep phase. Then simply add a little more weight in the final two weeks. I know I sound like a broken record but, when in doubt, it's best to use less weight, not more. You have a lifetime of training in front of you, so take your time.

Remember, too, in this strength phase it's important to do smooth, fast repetitions and pause briefly between reps to let the pump subside. Lifting faster is important because it activates more contractile fibers, especially the fast-twitch fibers which increase in size (hypertrophy) more than do the slower contracting fibers. Nevertheless, you should never jerk or throw the weight. Lift fast, but don't let momentum do the work for the muscle. Always stay in control of the weight.

Actually, the weight will be heavy enough so that it won't move very fast. Nevertheless, if you *think* about lifting explosively, you'll trigger more muscle fibers even if the weight doesn't move particularly fast. So think speed, controlled speed.

Finally, in this strength phase, where the heaviest weights are used, warm-up becomes even more important. Do as many warm-up sets as it takes to prepare your muscles for each work set. Again, I suggest that you do a rep or two with the weight you are going to use in the work set. This gives you the feel of the weight, and gets you ready to do your best. You've spent eight weeks getting ready for this phase. Don't blow it by injuring yourself. Warm-up properly!

DAY TWO
Treadmill — Comfortable

Brief General Warm-Up: Same as before

Time	Speed	Grade	Effort
1 Minute	3.30 mph	0 Percent	Warm-Up
1	"	3	"
1	"	5	"
1	"	7	"
1	"	9	"
1	"	11	"
1	"	13	"
1	"	15	"
1	"	17	"
1	"	19	"
1	"	21	"
1	"	23	"
2	"	25	Work Period
4	"	10	Relief Interval
1	"	15	Transition
1	"	20	"
1	"	25	Work Period
1	3.50	23	"
4	3.30	10	Relief Interval
1	"	15	Transition
1	"	20	"
1	3.50	25	Work Period
2	3.30	10	Relief Interval
1	"	17.5	Transition
1	3.50	25	Work Period
2	3.30	10	Relief Interval
1	"	17.5	Transition
1	3.50	25	Work Period
1	3.30	5	Cool-Down
1	"	0	"
1	2.80	"	"

40 minutes total

5-10 minutes: Brief General Cool-Down and Stretch

Here the hill (or gradient) is steeper, but also shorter. The top grade is now 25%, and the work periods are shortened to one and two minutes. In addition, the relief intervals are now twice as long as the work periods.

Runners might compare this workout to doing 440- and 220-yard interval sprints. The main difference is that the steep incline here allows you to walk rather than run. The effect is basically the same, but obviously walking is easier on the joints. That's why I like training on the treadmill.

Some treadmills, I realize, do not elevate to 25% (I use 25% because that's the maximum grade used by The Cooper Clinic in its testing protocol). If your treadmill doesn't elevate to 25%, you may find it necessary to use a faster speed than shown above. As was the case in the earlier treadmill workouts, it's up to you to adjust the speed and grade to make this workout "comfortable" for you. Stick to the one- and two-minute work periods, however. They're the distinguishing feature separating the strength-phase treadmill workouts from those in the other phases.

As I promised, after the very hard treadmill workout last week (Week Eight), the difficulty level here is scaled back considerably. The intensity will increase each week, however, and become "very hard" again in the fourth week of this phase. That means, of course, that the speed and grade you select for this week should allow plenty of room for improvement as the phase unfolds. Again, make sure that — for you — this workout is comfortable.

DAY THREE
Walk

DAY FOUR
Weight Workout B — 8 Reps — 90%

DAY FIVE
Air-Dyne — Easy

Brief General Warm-Up: Same as before

Time	Load	Effort
1 Minute	2.00 mph	Warm-Up
2	3.00	"
2	4.00	"
2	5.00	Work Period
4	3.00	Relief Interval
1	5.50	Work Period

1	4.50	Work Period
4	3.00	Relief Interval
1	6.00	Work Period
2	3.00	Relief Interval
1	6.00	Work Period
4	3-2	Cool-Down

25 minutes total

5-10 minutes: Brief General Cool-Down and Stretch

Be patient. Enjoy the "easy" pace of this workout. As promised earlier, the Air-Dyne workouts in the next training routine will challenge your capacity.

What's more, the high level of difficulty in the weight and treadmill sessions during this strength phase make the easy days all the more important. So cool it in this workout.

DAY SIX
Walk

DAY SEVEN
Rest

WEEK 10

Day One: Weight Workout B — 8 Reps — 100%

This is one of the dress-rehearsal workouts enroute to setting a new personal best. Do eight repetitions with 100% of your previous maximum. Don't try to exceed your previous best, however. You'll have that opportunity in Week 12.

DAY TWO
Treadmill — Somewhat Hard

Brief General Warm-Up: Same as before

Time	Speed	Grade	Effort
1 Minute	3.30 mph	0 Percent	Warm-Up
1	"	3	"
1	"	5	"
1	"	7	"
1	"	9	"
1	"	11	"
1	"	13	"
1	"	15	"
1	"	17	"

Day Two (cont.)

1	3.30	19	Warm-Up
1	"	21	"
1	"	23	"
1	"	25	Work Period
1	3.50	"	"
4	3.30	10	Relief Interval
1	"	15	Transition
1	"	20	"
1	3.50	25	Work Period
1	3.70	23	"
4	3.30	10	Relief Interval
1	3.50	15	Transition
1	3.70	20	"
1	"	25	Work Period
2	3.30	10	Relief Interval
1	3.50	17.5	Transition
1	3.70	25	Work Period
2	3.30	10	Relief Interval
1	3.50	17.5	Transition
1	3.70	25	Work Period
1	3.30	5	Cool-Down
1	"	0	"
1	2.80	"	"

40 minutes total

5-10 minutes: Brief General Cool-Down and Stretch

The top speed here is increased to 3.70 miles per hour. That upgrades this workout to "somewhat hard." Set the speed and grade to allow room for two more increases. If that means you need to adjust downward at this point or even repeat this workout, don't hesitate to do so.

Psychologically, it's important that you don't fail in the workouts at the end of the phase. If adjustments are necessary, it's better to make them now rather than later. After you've completed a few training cycles, you'll be better able to gauge your capacity. Look on this first training cycle as a break-in period, a time to get the bugs out of your training system.

DAY THREE
Walk

DAY FOUR
Weight Workout A — 8 Reps — 90%

This is your chance to back off a little in Weight Workout A before pushing on to a new personal record in this workout next week.

DAY FIVE
Air-Dyne — Easy

(Same as Week Nine)

DAY SIX
Walk

DAY SEVEN
Rest

Adjust your workouts to insure that your training experience is continually positive. *Photo by Chris Lund.*

WEEK 11

Day One: Weight Workout A — 8 Reps — 105%

This is the big day! Think of it as a competition with yourself. You've done your homework. You're ready. Now go for it!

Positive feedback, as explained earlier, is essential to maintaining motivation. You need to see results from your training. That's why the periodization system works so well. Done properly, you never undertake more than you can accomplish. Each exercise session is designed to produce a sense of achievement. You improve gradually from week to week and, finally, at the end of the phase or cycle, you achieve a peak performance. Again, for the sake of your motivation, it's very important that the sequence works this way.

That's why I keep encouraging you to adjust the difficulty of your workouts. I don't want you to stumble at the end of the phase. Make sure that you fine tune your training for success.

This takes a little practice, of course. You have to learn how your body responds to training. After a training cycle or two, however, you'll have it down pat. And when you do, you'll be able to look forward to a lifetime of successful training.

Remember, success breeds success. Adjust your workouts to ensure that your training experience is continually positive. That's the key. That's what keeps you training... and improving!

DAY TWO
Treadmill — Hard

Brief General Warm-Up: Same as before

Time	Speed	Grade	Effort
1 Minute	3.30 mph	0 Percent	Warm-Up
1	,,	3	,,
1	,,	5	,,
1	,,	7	,,
1	,,	9	,,
1	,,	11	,,
1	,,	13	,,
1	,,	15	,,
1	,,	17	,,
1	,,	19	,,
1	,,	21	,,
1	,,	23	,,
1	3.50	25	Work Period
1	3.70	,,	,,
4	3.30	10	Relief Interval

1	3.30	15	Transition
1	3.50	20	"
1	3.70	25	Work Period
1	3.90	23	"
4	3.30	10	Relief Interval
1	3.50	15	Transition
1	3.70	20	"
1	3.90	25	Work Period
2	3.30	10	Relief Interval
1	3.60	17.5	Transition
1	3.90	25	Work Period
2	3.30	10	Relief Interval
1	3.60	17.5	Transition
1	3.90	25	Work Period
1	3.30	5	Cool-Down
1	"	0	"
1	2.80	"	"

40 minutes total

5-10 minutes: Brief General Cool-Down and Stretch

This is the second-to-last treadmill workout. It should be "hard," but not so hard that you become apprehensive about the "very hard" workout scheduled for next week.

As I emphasized in connection with yesterday's weight work-out, it's critical that you pace yourself properly through the course of this phase. With a little practice, you'll be able to coordinate your training so you'll peak at the end of the phase. Ideally, you should bump up against your limit next week... and not before. So plan carefully. Make this workout a confidence builder for your final treadmill session next week.

DAY THREE
Walk

DAY FOUR
Weight Workout B — 8 Reps — 95%

This is the final tune-up on Weight Workout B. Next week you hit your peak.

DAY FIVE
Air-Dyne — Comfortable

Brief General Warm-Up: Same as before

Day Five (cont.)

Time	Load	Effort
1 Minute	2.00 mph	Warm-Up
2	3.50	,,
2	4.50	,,
2	5.50	Work Period
4	3.30	Relief Interval
1	6.00	Work Period
1	5.00	,,
4	3.00	Relief Interval
1	6.50	Work Period
2	3.00	Relief Interval
1	6.50	Work Period
4	3-2	Cool-Down

25 minutes total

5-10 minutes: Brief General Cool-Down and Stretch

DAY SIX
Walk

DAY SEVEN
Rest

WEEK 12

Day One: Weight Workout B — 8 Reps — 105%

You did it! Congratulations!

If everything went according to plan, you set a new personal record and should be elated at this point. You did what you set out to do. Success is yours.

You're stronger now. That means you can realistically expect to reach new heights in your next endurance phase. The fact that you can lift more for eight reps means that you've developed the base of strength necessary to lift more for 20 repetitions as well. As explained in Chapter Five, endurance has a strength component. So, you see, by sequencing your training like this and improving from phase to phase, you're setting yourself up for a continuing cycle of success. Again, that's the beauty of periodization.

But now let's switch our attention to tomorrow's treadmill workout, which is your immediate challenge.

You need to see results from your training. Remember, success breeds success. *Photo by Guy Appelman.*

DAY TWO
Treadmill — Very Hard

Brief General Warm-Up: Same as before

Time	Speed	Grade	Effort
1 Minute	3.30 mph	0 Percent	Warm-Up
1	"	3	"
1	"	5	"
1	"	7	"
1	"	9	"
1	"	11	"
1	"	13	"
1	"	15	"
1	"	17	"
1	"	19	"
1	3.50	21	"
1	"	23	"
1	3.70	25	Work Period
1	3.90	"	"
4	3.30	10	Relief Interval
1	3.50	15	Transition
1	3.70	20	"
1	3.90	25	Work Period
1	4.10	23 (Jog)	"
4	3.30	10	Relief Interval
1	3.70	15	Transition
1	3.90	20	"
1	4.10	25 (Jog)	Work Period
2	3.30	10	Relief Interval
1	3.70	17.5	Transition
1	4.10	25 (Jog)	Work Period
2	3.30	10	Relief Interval
1	3.70	17.5	Transition
1	4.10	25 (Jog)	Work Period
1	3.30	5	Cool-Down
1	"	0	"
1	2.80	"	"

40 minutes total

5-10 minutes: Brief General Cool-Down and Stretch

Great effort! Congratulations again! Now it's time for a couple of easy weeks. But first let's finish the strength phase with some lighter workouts.

DAY THREE
Walk

DAY FOUR
Weight Workout A — 8 Reps — 95%

This will be duck soup after last week's record-breaking session.

DAY FIVE
Air-Dyne — Comfortable

(Same as Week 11)

DAY SIX
Walk

DAY SEVEN
Rest

THE END-OF-CYCLE RECOVERY PERIOD

Now you need a break! You don't want to plunge back into hard training right after peaking. Complete rest, however, is not the best way to recover. That, of course, is why I recommend walking on off-days. This is the time for what exercise physiologists call "active rest."

That means you should stay active, but do something different and easy. Give your battery an opportunity to recharge. I usually walk a lot, play around with some different weight exercises, and maybe ride my trail bicycle in the foothills near my house. Do whatever appeals to you. After a couple of weeks, you'll be itching to get back to regular workouts.

If you're relatively new to training or just getting back in shape, you'll probably want to repeat the A-B, Whole-Body Balanced Routine we have just completed, except that you'll make the workouts fractionally harder because your endurance and strength have improved. More advanced trainers, who often require higher initial volumes and intensities, as well as more frequent change, will be ready to try the Push-Pull Split, Balanced Routine and the Three-Way, Short-Phase Routines.

Because the foundation information has already been presented in our detailed description of the A-B, Whole-Body Balanced Routine, we can dispense with the day-by-day format used up to now and focus, in a general way, on the main distinguishing features of these other two routines.

Take a break at the end of the training cycle. Do something different *and* easy. Give your battery an opportunity to recharge before
you plunge into the next training cycle. *Photo by Guy Appelman.*

THE PUSH-PULL SPLIT, BALANCED ROUTINE

In this routine, the rate of change increases. The phase changes six times in 12 weeks, or every two weeks. As you'd expect, that means the overall intensity level is higher as well. In the last routine, the intensity of the weight workouts started at 90% and dropped to 80% on easy days. Here the weight workouts never fall below 95% intensity.

The longer you train, as mentioned earlier, the faster your body adapts to the stress of exercise. This means that, in order to keep improving, you must change the stress more frequently. This routine does that in a logical manner. What's more, the frequent changes make you *want* to train. Every workout is an exciting, new challenge.

As in the last routine, weights and aerobics are stressed equally. "Push-pull split" in the name actually refers to the weight training portion. The body is divided (split) into pushing and pulling muscles, and they're trained separately with weights. It just so happens, however, that the rest of the routine also involves pushing and pulling. The aerobic sessions are divided between the Air-Dyne, the stationary bicycle with push-pull arm action used in the first routine, and the Concept II rower (rowing, of course, involves pulling with the

What's more, the frequent changes in your routine will make you want to train. Every workout is an exciting, new challenge.

arms and pushing with the legs). As promised, the main stress is on the Air-Dyne. The rowing sessions, like the Air-Dyne workouts in the last routine, are always relatively easy (but they become the hardest sessions in a portion of the next routine).

The day-to-day training sequence is the same as in the first routine: weights on Day One, aerobics on Day Two, walk on Day Three, weights on Day Four, aerobics on Day Five, walk on Day Six and rest on Day Seven. Since they are the same as before, I won't refer to the walk and rest days again. Omitting walk and rest days, here is the 12-week training cycle:

THE ENDURANCE PHASE
Weights — 20 Reps; Aerobics — 10-Min. Intervals

Week One
Weights — Push — 95%
Air-Dyne — Somewhat Hard
Weights — Pull — 95%
Rower — Easy

The longer you train the faster your body adapts to the stress of exercise. This means that, in order to keep improving, you must change the stress more frequently. *Photo by Guy Appelman.*

Week Two
Weights — Push — 100%
Air-Dyne — Hard
Weights — Pull — 100%
Rower — Comfortable

THE STRENGTH-AND-ENDURANCE PHASE
Weights — 12 Reps; Aerobics — 5-Min. Intervals

Week Three
Weights — Push — 95%
Air-Dyne — Somewhat Hard
Weights — Pull — 95%
Rower — Easy

Week Four
Weights — Push — 100%
Air-Dyne — Hard
Weights — Pull — 100%
Rower — Comfortable

THE STRENGTH PHASE
Weights — 8 Reps; Aerobics — 1-2 Min. Intervals

Week Five
Weights — Push — 95%
Air-Dyne — Somewhat Hard
Weights — Pull — 95%
Rower — Easy

Week Six
Weights — Push — 100%
Air-Dyne — Hard
Weights — Pull — 100%
Rower — Comfortable

THE ENDURANCE PHASE
Weights — 20 Reps; Aerobics — 10-Min. Intervals

Week Seven
Weights — Push — 100%
Air-Dyne — Hard
Weights — Pull — 100%
Rower — Comfortable

Week Eight
Weights — Push — 105%
Air-Dyne — Very Hard
Weights — Pull — 105%
Rower — Somewhat Hard

THE STRENGTH AND ENDURANCE PHASE
Weights — 12 Reps; Aerobics — 5-Min. Intervals

Week Nine
Weights — Push — 100%
Air-Dyne — Hard
Weights — Pull — 100%
Rower — Comfortable

Week 10
Weights — Push — 105%
Air-Dyne — Very Hard
Weights — Pull — 105%
Rower — Somewhat Hard

THE STRENGTH PHASE
Weights — 8 Reps; Aerobics — 1-2 Min. Intervals

Week 11
Weights — Push — 100%
Air-Dyne — Hard
Weights — Pull — 100%
Rower — Comfortable

Week 12
Weights — Push — 105%
Air-Dyne — Very Hard
Weights — Pull — 105%
Rower — Somewhat Hard

END-OF-CYCLE RECOVERY PERIOD
One or Two Weeks

*****

Dividing the body into pushing and pulling muscles in the weight portion of this routine allows time and energy to train each body part more completely. That's the purpose of a split routine; it permits you to concentrate more on each body part, do more sets or train each muscle group from more angles.

Here the pushing muscles — thighs, calves, chest, shoulders and triceps — are trained on Day One and the pulling muscles — lower back, leg biceps (or hamstrings), upper back, biceps and waist — on Day Four. Both weight workouts are hard.

It may seem like we've abandoned the hard-day/easy-day principle, but we really haven't. The hard-easy idea is at work here, but in a different form. The pulling muscles rest on push day, and the pushing muscles rest on pull day. So even though there are no easy weight sessions in this routine, the hard-easy principle is, nevertheless, in effect.

In the previous routine, each body part was trained twice, once hard and a second time with less intensity. Here each muscle group is trained hard, but only once a week. Is that enough? Yes, for reasons I'll explain, I think it is.

First, there is some overlap in the two workouts. As you'll see, the Squat is included in the pushing workout and the Deadlift in the pulling session. Both of these exercises, as noted earlier, work the thighs, hips and lower back. So, in effect, the biggest and most powerful muscles in the body are worked twice each week. Plus, in the previous routine, each training session included only one

Both bodybuilders and endurance athletes are training less now — and getting better in the bargain. They are training less, but harder. *Photo by Bill Reynolds.*

exercise for each body part. As you'll soon see, the push-pull split allows us to include two or three exercises per body part. The end result is that, in this routine, we do as many or more exercises for each body part as we did before. We simply do them all in one training session. And remember, in this routine both training sessions are hard. So, in the final analysis, each muscle group is trained harder than before. Again, that's the purpose of a split routine.

Moreover, this routine is in tune with the less-is-more trend discussed in Chapter Five. Both body-builders and endurance athletes are training less now — and getting better in the bargain. They're training less, but harder. As you'll recall, research shows that training success depends more on intensity than anything else. What this routine sacrifices in frequency, it more than makes up for in increased intensity. After you try this routine, I believe you'll agree that training each body part once a week, as it's done here, is indeed enough.

What this routine sacrifices in frequency, it more than makes up for in increased intensity.

Now let's look at the specific exercises included in each weight session. First, here's the weight workout for Day One:

PUSHING MUSCLES

Brief General Warm-Up:	Same as before
Barbell Squat:	warm-up and one work set
Leg Extension:	"
Calf Raise on Leg Press:	"
Seated Calf Raise:	"
Bench Press:	"
Incline Dumbbell Press:	"
Crossover Pulley Fly:	"
Standing Barbell Press:	"
Dumbbell Lateral Raise:	"
Dumbbell Behind-Neck Triceps Extension:	"
Brief General Cool-Down:	Same as General Warm-Up

And here's the weight workout to be done on Day Four:

PULLING MUSCLES

Brief General Warm-Up:	Same as before
Deadlift:	warm up and one work set
Leg Curl:	"
Lat Pulldown (front):	"

Bent-Over Barbell Row:	warm up and one work set
Behind-Neck Lat Pulldown:	"
Dumbbell Shrug:	"
Barbell Curl:	"
Bent-Knee Sit-Up:	"
Hip Curl (see photos page 164):	"
One-Arm Dumbbell Side Bend:	"
Brief General Cool-Down:	Same as General Warm-Up

As mentioned earlier, we won't go through this routine on a day-by-day basis. The approach in each phase is already familiar to you: 20 reps and relatively light weights in the endurance phase, 12 reps and moderate weights in the strength-endurance phase, and eight repetitions and relatively heavy weights in the strength phase. As already noted, the main change from the previous routine is that the phase changes every two weeks. In this routine, you go through all three phases *twice*. Because the phases are only half as long, there's less time to increase the weight gradually. So, of necessity, the initial poundages are higher.

In the first three phases, the intensity increases from 95% in the first week to 100% in the second week. In other words, in the first six weeks, you equal your best in all three phases. In the final six weeks, you equal your best in each phase, again, in the first week of each phase, then move on to new PR's in the final week. You'll see what I mean as we actually go through the routine in detail.

Note that the pattern is the same as before: you push for a while, back off, change weight and repetitions, and then push again, this time at a slightly higher level than before. It's a system structured for success. You don't overstay your welcome in a phase. Before that can happen, you move on to the next phase. Constant change makes it work. You experience one success after another. And that keeps you motivated.

I had not used the push-pull split for a while, but as I was writing this, I decided to try it again. Actually, I repeat almost all of the workouts as I write about them. It helps me analyze and explain them better.

As I put on my workout clothes, I made a mental note of the fact that I was looking forward to doing a push workout. Actually, I almost always feel that way before a change of routine. I think most people feel a sense of excitement and challenge before doing a new workout.

Just like you will be doing, I started with the endurance phase. Frankly, I always feel a little hesitant about doing 20 repetitions in the Squat. I know it's going to be hard. I felt better, however, knowing that I would be using 5% less weight than my recent best.

I've been doing the Barbell Squat for 40 years now, and there's no getting around it, Squats are hard! Nevertheless, in my opinion, there's no better exercise. I plan to keep squatting as long as I can. *Photo by Guy Appelman.*

That's a substantial reduction on a big muscle exercise like the Squat. I did a couple of warm-up sets and then loaded the bar for my work set. It went great! I did 22 reps, two more than planned. That gave me confidence that I'll have no trouble doing 100% the next week.

In recent workouts I'd been doing only one thigh exercise (12 reps). But as you know, the push workout allows time for two quadriceps exercises. So I moved on to the second thigh exercise, Leg Extensions. Whenever I switch to 20 reps, even though I've done it many times, I'm always shocked by the difference. On the 12th rep of the Leg Extensions my thighs started to burn. By the 20th rep it felt like they were on fire!

Yes, 20-rep sets really are a different ball game, especially on the second exercise for the same body part. That pain from the lactic acid buildup isn't pleasant, but it signals you're really pushing the muscle to the maximum and stimulating progress. Experienced bodybuilders will know what I mean when I say, "It hurts so good."

I had been doing the Barbell Bench Press and Incline Dumbbell Press in my previous workouts, so the only difference I noticed on those exercises was that it felt good to do 20 reps for a change. I liked the extra pump.

However, the next exercise, the Crossover Pulley Fly for the chest, had not been part of my training program for a while. Because of a biceps injury, I'd stopped doing Crossover Pulley movements some months before. The injury had healed, however, and I was ready to resume Crossover exercises.

I did the Crossover Pulley Fly in a kneeling position with my upper body at a 45-degree angle (see photos next two pages). I concentrated on contracting my lower pectoral muscles hard at the end of the movement. It felt so good that I did 25 reps!

The new exercise and the extra reps really did the job, because the next morning my lower pecs were sore. The day after that they were *really* sore. That's the two-day lag. It's a sure sign that I activated muscle fibers that hadn't been used for a while.

Yes, based on my experience, I think you're going to enjoy the push-pull split.

(If you don't have access to a crossover pulley, substitute the Dumbbell Fly in your routine. Use a decline bench; you'll find the exercise works the lower chest much like the pulley movement just described. Maintain a bend in your elbows to keep the stress on the chest.)

This is the Crossover Pulley Fly exercise that made my lower pecs so sore. *Photo by Guy Appelman.*

The Crossover Pulley Fly can also be done in a standing position. Note how I am stretching the chest muscles at the beginning of the movement and contracting them at the end.

*Photos by
Guy Appelman.*

Now let's look at the Air-Dyne workout you'll be doing on Day Two. As in the past, I've indicated my own training loads on a pre-1989 Air-Dyne for illustration purposes. This time, however, I won't set out each workout separately. I've prepared three tables to show the workout pattern in each phase. The first table is for the endurance phase. It shows the load variations as I move from "somewhat hard" to "hard" and, finally, "very hard."

DAY TWO: AIR-DYNE
The Endurance Phase

Brief General Warm-Up: Same as before

Time	Load			Effort
	"Somewhat Hard" (Week 1)	"Hard" (Weeks 2 & 7)	"Very Hard" (Week 8)	
5 Min.	2-4	2-4.5	2-5.0	Warm-Up
10	4.50	5.00	5.50	Work Period
5	3.50	3.50	3.50	Relief Interval
2	4.50	5.00	5.50	Work Period
2	5.00	5.50	6.00	"
2	4.00	4.50	5.00	"
2	4.75	5.25	5.75	"
2	4.25	4.75	5.25	"
5	3-1	3-1	3-1	Cool-Down

35 minutes total

5-10 minutes: Brief General Cool-Down and Stretch

As you can see, in the endurance phase, there are two 10-minute work periods. The first one is done at a steady pace and, for variety, the second work period changes every two minutes.

Duplicating the pattern of the weight workouts, the intensity moves from "somewhat hard" (Week One) to "hard" (Week Two). When the endurance phase continues in Week Seven, you'll repeat the "hard" session, then move to "very hard" in Week Eight. As the next table shows, the intensity level escalates the same way in the strength-and-endurance phase (and later in the strength phase as well).

DAY TWO: AIR-DYNE
The Strength-and-Endurance Phase

Brief General Warm-Up: Same as before

Time	Load			Effort
	"Somewhat Hard" (Week 3)	"Hard" (Weeks 4 & 9)	"Very Hard" (Wk 10)	
5 Min.	2-4.5	2-5.0	2-5.5	Warm-Up
5	5.50	6.00	6.50	Work Period
5	3.50	3.50	3.50	Relief Interval
1	5.50	6.00	6.50	Work Period
1	6.00	6.50	7.00	"
1	5.00	5.50	6.00	"
1	5.75	6.25	6.75	"
1	5.25	5.75	6.25	"
5	3.50	3.50	3.50	Relief Interval
5	5.00	5.50	6.00	Work Period
5	3-1	3-1	3-1	Cool-Down

35 minutes total

5-10 minutes: Brief General Cool-Down and Stretch

As was the case in the A-B, Whole-Body Balanced Routine, the Air-Dyne workouts in the strength-and-endurance phase of this routine call for five-minute work periods. Here, however, the Air-Dyne is no longer the easy session; it's the hard aerobic workout. That, of course, means that the intensity levels are upgraded. Workouts that earlier were "easy" and "comfortable" are now "somewhat hard," "hard" and "very hard."

Like the treadmill workouts in the first routine, these Air-Dyne sessions are supposed *to challenge you!* Remember, the load numbers are mine and must be adjusted, up or down, to suit your level of fitness.

DAY TWO: AIR-DYNE
The Strength Phase

Brief General Warm-Up: Same as before

Time	Load			Effort
	"Somewhat Hard" (Week 5)	"Hard" (Weeks 6 & 11)	"Very Hard" (Wk 12)	
5 Min.	2-5	2-5	2-5	Warm-Up
2	6.00	6.50	7.00	Work Period
4	3.50	3.50	3.50	Relief Interval
1	7.00	7.50	8.00	Work Period
2	3.50	3.50	3.50	Relief Interval
1	7.00	7.50	8.00	Work Period

Day Two (cont.)

2	3.50	3.50	3.50	Relief Interval
1	7.00	7.50	8.00	Work Period
2	3.50	3.50	3.50	Relief Interval
2	5.50	6.00	6.50	Work Period
4	3.50	3.50	3.50	Relief Interval
1	6.50	7.00	7.50	Work Period
5	3-1	3-1	3-1	Cool-Down

32 minutes total

5-10 minutes: Brief General Cool-Down and Stretch

As was the case in the strength-phase treadmill workouts in the last routine, the short work periods in these Air-Dyne sessions are essentially sprints. They will turn your arms and legs — especially your legs — to jelly. To compensate, the relief periods in this phase are proportionally longer. That gives your muscles more time to get rid of lactic acid between work periods.

You definitely will be challenged, not bored with the Air-Dyne workouts in the strength phase. In fact, after the "very hard" workout in Week 12, you'll need a week or two to recover before starting the next training cycle.

But, first, let's look at the "easy," "comfortable" and "somewhat hard" rowing workouts you'll be doing each week on Day Five. They'll get you ready for some hard "pieces" (rowing terminology for work periods) in the last routine.

DAY FIVE: ROWER
The Endurance Phase

Brief General Warm-Up: Same as before

Time	**Pace**			**Effort**
			"Somewhat	
	"Easy"	"Comfortable"	Hard"	
	(Week 1)	(Weeks 2 & 7)	(Week 8)	
5 Min.	2:30	2:30	2:30	Warm-Up
10	2:10	2:05	2:00	Work Period
5	2:30	2:30	2:30	Relief Interval
2	2:15	2:10	2:05	Work Period
2	2:20	2:15	2:10	"
2	2:10	2:05	2:00	"
2	2:17	2:12	2:07	"
2	2:13	2:08	2:03	"
5	2:30	2:30	2:30	Cool-Down

35 minutes total

5-10 minutes: Brief General Cool-Down and Stretch

As you probably gathered from my comments in Chapter Two, the Concept II Rowing Ergometer is another of my favorite aerobic exercise machines. Two things attract me to this piece of equipment. The first is the competitive aspect.

The electronic performance monitor on the Concept II rower makes it possible to precisely compare performances around the world. Competitions using this machine attract rowers from all over the globe. As mentioned earlier, the Concept II company compiles a world ranking each year, an ordered list of personal bests for 2500 meters rowed on their machine. Times are grouped into 10-year age classes for both men and women. The ranking also categorizes competitors by weight, denoting men and women above and below 160 and 135 pounds respectively. In short, not only

The Concept II rower allows you to compare yourself with rowers of similar age, sex and weight from around the world.

does the Concept II rower allow competition with oneself, it also allows you to compare yourself with rowers of similar age, sex and weight from around the world.

This photo conveys some of the concentration and effort involved in a high-level effort on the rower. Look at the grimace on my face! This picture was snapped by my wife, Carol, during the personal-record row described in Chapter Two, after I was inspired by the performance of the wonderful woman rower in Denver.

The other thing I find particularly appealing about indoor rowing is that it's an ideal sport for someone interested in both strength and endurance. It requires power (especially in the legs and back) *and* endurance.

As a former Olympic-style weightlifter, I find that the rowing motion reminds me of the Barbell Clean where the weight is lifted from the floor to shoulder level in one motion. On the Concept II rower you start pulling with your legs and hips, the strongest muscles in the body, then your lower back muscles, the next strongest, kick in and finally you end up pulling with your lats, traps and arms. It's a long and smooth, but powerful, movement. There's no undue stress on the joints. It feels good.

I won't kid you, however. A high-level effort on the rower, like any other endurance activity, causes pain and discomfort. "(An all-out 2500-meter row) is comparable to running a 440-yard dash for two miles," a female coach at the 1990 World Indoor Rowing Championships told *The Wall Street Journal.* "A normal body shouldn't be put under such strain."

So you can see why I believe that indoor rowing may be the ultimate challenge for a person interested in strength and endurance. In any event, it's just the type of activity you need to stay motivated. The electronic performance monitor on the Concept II rower (and I'm sure on other rowers as well) provides the feedback that is so critical to maintaining your motivation. It gives you an exciting new challenge and tells you how you're doing — in relation to yourself and to others.

As in the case of the Air-Dyne, intensity on the Concept II rower is determined by your own effort. The harder and faster you row, the more resistance is provided by fan blades built into the fly wheel on which the monitor is mounted. The monitor translates the speed and power of your rowing stroke into pace.

In the table above, "pace" refers to the time it takes to row 500 meters. (Competitive on-the-water rowers often gauge their speed by timing themselves for a 500-meter interval.) This information is constantly displayed on the monitor, along with elapsed time and meters rowed. For example, if you row every stroke at a pace of 2:05 for 500 meters, your elapsed time will be 2:05. If you pick up your pace by 10 seconds, from 2:05 to 1:55, as shown on the monitor, you reduce your 500-meter time to 1:55. It's not at all complicated. You'll catch on fast.

When you study the table showing the rowing workouts in the endurance phase, you'll see that the pattern is almost the same as in the Air-Dyne workouts: a five-minute warm-up followed by two 10-minute work periods, separated by a relief interval. The pace varies every two minutes in the second work period, and the average pace is five seconds slower.

The only difference in these workouts and the Air-Dyne sessions is the intensity. Because rowing is the easy aerobic activity in this routine, the highest difficulty level in this training cycle is "somewhat hard." The rowing workouts are "easy" in Week One, "comfortable" in Weeks Two and Seven and, as mentioned, reach "somewhat hard" in the final week of the second endurance phase.

The pattern of intensity is basically the same in the other two phases. Here are the rowing workouts in the strength-and-endurance phase:

DAY FIVE: ROWER
The Strength-and-Endurance Phase

Brief General Warm-Up: Same as before

Time	Pace			Effort
	"Easy" (Week 3)	"Comfortable" (Weeks 4 & 9)	"Somewhat Hard" (Week 10)	
5 min.	2:30	2:30	2:30	Warm-Up
5	2:05	2:01	1:58	Work Period
5	2:30	2:30	2:30	Relief Interval
1	2:05	2:01	1:58	Work Period
1	2:01	1:57	1:54	"
1	2:09	2:05	2:02	"
1	2:03	1:59	1:56	"
1	2:07	2:03	2:00	"
5	2:30	2:30	2:30	Cool-Down

25 minutes total

5-10 minutes: Brief General Cool-Down & Stretch

The work periods in this phase are five minutes in length, same as in the Air-Dyne sessions. The only difference is that there are two, rather than three, work periods here. As a consequence, the total rowing time is 10 minutes less than the Air-Dyne sessions. As you'll recall, the easy workouts in the A-B, Whole-Body, Balanced routine were shorter as well.

Finally, here are the strength-phase rowing workouts:

DAY FIVE: ROWER
The Strength Phase

Brief General Warm-Up: Same as before

Time	Pace			Effort
	"Easy" (Week 5)	"Comfortable" (Weeks 6 & 11)	"Somewhat Hard" (Week 12)	
5 min.	2:30	2:30	2:30	Warm-Up
2	2:00	1:55	1:52	Work Period
4	2:30	2:30	2:30	Relief Interval
1	1:58	1:53	1:50	Work Period
1	2:02	1:57	1:54	"
4	2:30	2:30	2:30	Relief Interval
1	1:57	1:53	1:50	Work Period
2	2:30	2:30	2:30	Relief Interval
1	1:57	1:53	1:50	Work Period
4	2:30	2:30	2:30	Relief Interval

25 minutes total

5-10 minutes: Brief General Cool-Down & Stretch

That's it for the Push-Pull Split, Balanced Routine. Take a week or two of active rest, then you'll be ready for the Three-Way, Short-Phase Routine. With more variety and intensity, it's the most challenging of all.

218

This is another photo of the correct starting position for the Deadlift. It's also the starting position for the Barbell Clean where the
weight is lifted from the floor to shoulder level in one motion. You
can see the parallels between the Deadlift and the Barbell Clean,
which involve the legs and back so strongly, and rowing on an
indoor rowing machine. Rowing hard for 2500 meters is like doing
heavy Deadlifts or Cleans for 10 minutes straight. Yes, indeed,
indoor rowing is an exciting challenge for anyone interested in
strength *and* endurance. *Photo by Mike Neveux.*

THE THREE-WAY, SHORT-PHASE ROUTINE

Three is the number to remember. In this routine, there are three whole-body weight workouts (A, B and C). In addition, the hard-day aerobic workout changes three times — first it's the rower, then the treadmill, then the Air-Dyne. Finally, all three phases (endurance, strength-endurance and strength) are repeated three times. Plus, a new phase, the unload phase, is introduced in this routine. And, yes, it's repeated three times, too.

The only thing that doesn't change is the intensity. Except for easy days (and the unload phase), all weight workouts are 100%, and all aerobic sessions are "hard."

Sounds complicated? Actually, it's not. The pattern of change is quite consistent and logical. To give you a bird's eye view, here's the whole 12-week training cycle (the daily training sequence is the same as before: Day One — Weights, Day Two — Aerobics, Day Three — Walk, Day Four — Weights, Day Five — Aerobics, Day Six — Walk, Day Seven — Rest).

WEEK ONE: THE ENDURANCE PHASE
Weights — 20 Reps; Aerobics — 10-Min. Intervals
Weights — A — 100%
Rower — Hard
Weights — B — 85%
Treadmill — Comfortable

WEEK TWO: STRENGTH-AND-ENDURANCE PHASE
Weights — 12 Reps; Aerobics — 5-Min. Intervals
Weights — A — 100%
Rower — Hard
Weights — B — 85%
Treadmill — Comfortable

WEEK THREE: THE STRENGTH PHASE
Weights — 8 Reps; Aerobics — 1-2 Min. Intervals
Weights — A — 100%
Rower — Hard
Weights — B — 85%
Treadmill — Comfortable

WEEK FOUR: THE UNLOAD PHASE
Weights — 12 Reps; Aerobics — 5-Min. Intervals
Weights — A — 75%
Rower — Easy
Weights — B — 75%
Treadmill — Easy

WEEK FIVE: THE ENDURANCE PHASE
Weights — 20 Reps; Aerobics — 10-Min. Intervals

Weights — B — 100%

Treadmill — Hard

Weights — C — 85%

Air-Dyne — Comfortable

WEEK SIX: STRENGTH-AND-ENDURANCE PHASE
Weights — 12 Reps; Aerobics — 5-Min. Intervals

Weights — B — 100%

Treadmill — Hard

Weights — C — 85%

Air-Dyne — Comfortable

WEEK SEVEN: THE STRENGTH PHASE
Weights — 8 Reps; Aerobics — 1-2 Min. Intervals

Weights — B — 100%

Treadmill — Hard

Weights — C — 85%

Air-Dyne — Comfortable

WEEK EIGHT: THE UNLOAD PHASE
Weights — 12 Reps; Aerobics — 5-Min. Intervals

Weights — B — 75%

Treadmill — Easy

Weights — C — 75%

Air-Dyne — Easy

WEEK NINE: THE ENDURANCE PHASE
Weights — 20 Reps; Aerobics — 10-Min. Intervals

Weights — C — 100%

Air-Dyne — Hard

Weights — A — 85%

Rower — Comfortable

WEEK 10: STRENGTH-AND-ENDURANCE PHASE
Weights — 12 Reps; Aerobics — 5-Min. Intervals

Weights — C — 100%

Air-Dyne — Hard

Weights — A — 85%

Rower — Comfortable

WEEK 11: THE STRENGTH PHASE
Weights — 8 Reps; Aerobics — 1-2 Min. Intervals

Weights — C — 100%

Air-Dyne — Hard

Weights — A — 85%

Rower — Comfortable

WEEK 12: THE UNLOAD PHASE
Weights — 12 Reps; Aerobics — 5-Min. Intervals
Weights — C — 75%
Air-Dyne — Easy
Weights — A — 75%
Rower — Easy

END-OF-CYCLE RECOVERY PERIOD
One Week

*****

As you can see, the rate of change peaks in this routine. The phase changes weekly (four times as fast as the first routine and twice as often as the last routine). What's more, the weight and aerobic workouts rotate every four weeks. The overall effect is that the body is forced to constantly adapt and grow stronger.

In addition to more frequent change, greater intensity is required for continued progress when you have reached the advanced stage of training. You get that here as well. As noted earlier, the main weight and aerobic sessions are always hard. Nevertheless, the hard-easy principle keeps you from crossing over into the exhaustion stage. To prevent that, the second weight and aerobic sessions each week are done with less intensity. Plus,

This fast-paced, high-intensity routine brings you to the brink of overtraining, but doesn't let you fall in. *Photo by Chris Lund.*

every fourth week is an unload phase in which the intensity is "easy."

The bottom line is that this fast-paced, high-intensity routine brings you to the brink of overtraining, but doesn't let you fall in.

Again, there are three weight workouts. The whole body is trained in each session, but from different angles. Here are the A, B and C workouts:

WEIGHT WORKOUT A

Brief General Warm-Up:	Same as before
Barbell Squat:	warm-up and one work set
Leg Curl:	,,
Calf Raise on Leg Press:	,,
Seated Long Cable Row:	,,
Dumbbell Bench Press:	,,
Behind-Neck Barbell Press:	,,
Triceps Dumbbell Kickback:	,,
Barbell Curl:	,,
Bent-Knee Sit-Up (on incline board):	,,
Dumbbell Side Bend:	,,
Brief General Cool-Down:	Same as General Warm-Up

WEIGHT WORKOUT B

Brief General Warm-Up:	Same as before
Deadlift:	warm-up and one work set
Leg Extension:	,,
Standing Calf Raise:	,,
Behind-Neck Lat Pulldown:	,,
Incline Barbell Press:	,,
Dumbbell Side Lateral Raise:	,,
Narrow-Grip Bench Press:	,,
Preacher-Bench Barbell Curl:	,,
Hip Curl	,,
Twisting Sit-Up (on incline board):	,,
Brief General Cool-Down:	Same as General Warm-Up

WEIGHT WORKOUT C

Brief General Warm-Up:	Same as before
Leg Press:	warm-up and one work set
Back Hyperextension (on bench):	,,
Seated Calf-Raise:	,,
Narrow-Grip Lat Pulldown:	,,
Crossover Pulley Fly:	,,
Dumbbell Press on Steep Incline Bench:	,,
Dumbbell Behind-Neck Triceps Extension:	

Weight Workout C (continued)

Dumbbell Curl on Incline Bench:	warm-up and one work set
Hanging Leg Raise (use ankle weights if necessary):	,,
Twisting Ab Crunch (with feet over bench):	,,
Brief General Cool-Down:	Same as General Warm-Up

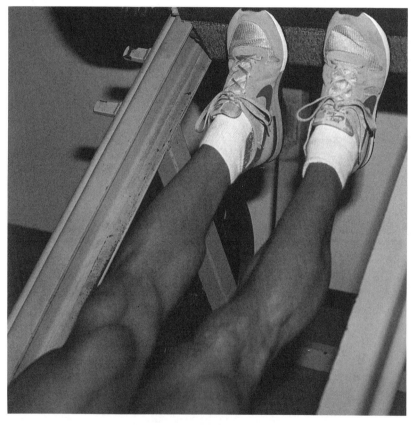

The Calf Raise on Leg Press, which is included in weight workout A, is my favorite exercise for the lower legs. There's no strain on the lower back, and you can get a good stretch at the bottom and a great contraction at the top. If you don't have access to a leg press machine, substitute One-Leg Calf Raises. Hold a dumbbell in your hand for added resistance, if necessary, and elevate your heels by standing on a step or block of wood to allow for a full stretch at the beginning of the movement. *Photo by Guy Appelman.*

The advantage of doing three separate whole-body weight workouts is much the same as doing a split routine. It permits you to train each muscle group from three different angles. It also prevents overtraining and possible injury from doing the same exercises repeatedly. Plus, as indicated earlier, changing workouts prevents the body from getting accustomed to the particular stress, thus slowing progress.

It's also important to note that rotation from phase to phase, as it's done in this routine, allows the body to adapt gradually. While the A workout exercises are done at 100% intensity during the first four weeks, the B workout exercises are performed with only 85% intensity; that prepares the muscles for maximum stress in the second four weeks. The C workout exercises are broken in the same way during Weeks Five through Eight, and then done with

Seated Long-Cable Rows are also included in weight workout A. Stretch the upper back at the start of the movement and pull with your lats, not your arms; keep lower back involvement to a minimum. If you don't have access to this apparatus, any rowing motion (barbell or dumbbell) can be substituted. *Photo by Guy Appelman.*

maximum intensity in the final four weeks. As I said earlier, it's a logical progression. I think you'll enjoy this routine.

Don't forget to change the weight and reps each week. Use relatively light weights and do 20-rep work sets in the endurance phase (Weeks One, Five and Nine). In the strength and endurance phase (Weeks Two, Six and 10) use moderate weights and 12 reps. In Weeks Three, Seven and 11 (the strength phase) use relatively heavy weight and do only eight reps. Finally, every fourth week (Weeks Four, Eight and 12) drop down to 75% intensity and do mid-range reps (12).

Finally, as you read on, you may be wondering why the intensity level in this routine never exceeds 100% (in other words, why you never try to exceed your previous maximum). In the first two routines, the weight workouts started at less than 100% intensity and increased gradually to 105% at the end of the training cycle. Here, however, the phases are too short to increase the load. The intensity starts and ends at 100%. What that does, essentially, is prepare you for new PR's in the next training cycle.

Think of this routine as a high-intensity springboard for later muscle gains. It pushes you hard, and then lets up for a few weeks to give your body time to recuperate. . . and gather strength. This routine gets you ready for a bounce to new highs in the next training cycle.

*****

Weights, of course, make up only half of this routine. The other

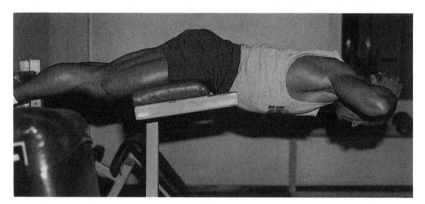

The Back Hyperextension exercise is the lower back movement included in weight workout C. Let your upper body hang down over the end of a bench, and then raise up to the position shown (don't arch your back at the top). If you don't have a Hyperextension bench, ask a training partner to hold your feet down. *Photo by Guy Appelman.*

half consists of sessions on the rower, the treadmill and the Air-Dyne. The rower receives the main focus early on, then it's the treadmill and, finally, the Air-Dyne.

The rower, as you know, was the easy aerobic session in the last routine. That prepared you for the hard rowing workouts you'll be doing during the first three weeks of this routine. The treadmill, which was the main aerobic activity in the first routine, is reintroduced here. It plays a secondary role to the rower at first, then becomes the hard-day session in the middle of the routine when the Air-Dyne is reintroduced as the easy workout. The Air-Dyne becomes the hard session the last few weeks. As you can see, it's a logical rotation. After all, that's what periodization is: planned, progressive change.

The Hanging Leg Raise is the exercise for your lower abdominal muscles included in weight workout C. As in the Hip Curl, curl your hips up, hold briefly in the position shown here, and then lower slowly. Don't swing, because that takes the stress off the abdominal muscles. *Photo by Guy Appelman.*

Here are the rowing workouts to be done on Day Two of the first four weeks: ("Pace," you'll recall, refers to the time it takes to row 500 meters on the Concept II Rowing Ergometer).

WEEK ONE: DAY TWO
The Endurance Phase
Rower — Hard

Brief General Warm-Up: Same as before

Time	Pace	Effort
5 Minutes	2:30 (or so)	Warm-Up
10	1:57	Work Period
5	2:30	Relief Interval
2	2:02	Work Period
2	2:05	"
2	1:59	"

Think of the third routine as a high-intensity springboard for later muscles gains. It gets you ready for a bounce to new highs in the next training cycle. *Photo by Guy Appelman.*

2	2:04	Work Period
2	2:00	,,
5	2:30 (or so)	Cool-Down

35 minutes total

5-10 minutes: Brief General Cool-Down & Stretch

WEEK TWO: DAY TWO
The Strength and Endurance Phase
Rower — Hard

Brief General Warm-Up: Same as before

Time	Pace	Effort
5 Minutes	2:30 (or so)	Warm-Up
5	1:55	Work Period
5	2:30	Relief Interval
1	1:55	Work Period
1	1:58	,,
1	1:52	,,
1	1:57	,,
1	1:53	,,
5	2:30	Relief Interval
5	2:00	Work Period
5	2:30 (or so)	Cool-Down

30 minutes total

5-10 minutes: Brief General Cool-Down & Stretch

WEEK THREE:DAY TWO
The Strength Phase
Rower — Hard

Brief General Warm-Up: Same as before

Time	Pace	Effort
5 Minutes	2:30 (or so)	Warm-Up
2	1:51	Work Period
4	2:30	Relief Interval
1	1:48	Work Period
2	2:30	Relief Interval
1	1:48	Work Period
2	2:30	Relief Interval
1	1:48	Work Period
2	2:30	Relief Interval
1	1:53	Work Period
1	1:49	,,

Week Three: Day Two (cont.)

4	2:30	Relief Interval
1	1:48	Work Period
5	2:30 (or so)	Cool-Down

32 minutes total

5-10 minutes: Brief General Cool-Down & Stretch

WEEK FOUR: DAY TWO
The Unload Phase
Rower — Easy

Same as the "easy" (Week 3) rowing session in the strength-and-endurance phase of the second routine (see page 214).

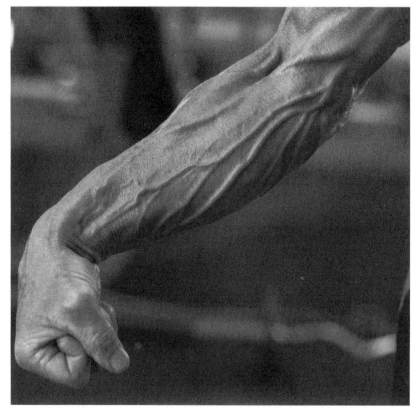

Photo by Chris Lund.

Here are the treadmill workouts to be done on the "easy" day (Day Five) of the first four weeks, and on the "hard" day (Day Two) of Weeks Five, Six and Seven: (the speeds and grades indicated are the ones I use; they must be adjusted, up or down, to suit your level of fitness).

WEEK ONE: DAY FIVE
The Endurance Phase
Treadmill — Comfortable

Same as the "comfortable" treadmill workout in Week One of the first routine (see page 159).

WEEK TWO: DAY FIVE
The Strength and Endurance Phase
Treadmill — Comfortable

Same as the "comfortable" treadmill workout in Week Five of the first routine (see page 177).

WEEK THREE: DAY FIVE
The Strength Phase
Treadmill — Comfortable

Same as the "comfortable" treadmill workout in Week Nine of the first routine (see page 189).

WEEK FOUR: DAY FIVE
The Unload Phase
Treadmill — Easy

Brief General Warm-Up: Same as before

Time	Speed	Grade	Effort
1 Minute	3.10 mph	0 Percent	Warm-Up
1	"	2	"
1	"	4	"
1	"	6	"
1	"	8	"
1	"	10	"
1	"	12	"
1	"	14	"
1	"	16	"
1	"	18	"
5	"	20	Work Period
2	2.50	10	Cool-Down

Week Four: Day Five (cont.)

2	2.50	5	Cool-Down
1	"	0	"

20 minutes total

5-10 minutes: Brief General Cool-Down & Stretch

WEEK FIVE: DAY TWO
The Endurance Phase
Treadmill — Hard

Brief General Warm-Up: Same as before

Time	Speed	Grade	Effort
1 Minute	3.30 mph	0 Percent	Warm-Up
1	"	1	"
1	"	3	"
1	"	5	"
1	"	7	"
1	3.50	"	"
1	"	9	"
1	"	11	"
1	"	13	"
1	3.70	"	"
10	"	15	Work Period
4	3.30	10	Relief Interval
1	3.50	12.5	Transition
2	3.70	15	Work Period
2	3.90	13	"
2	4.10	11 (Jog)	"
2	4.30	9 (Jog)	"
2	4.50	7 (Jog)	"
1	3.30	"	Cool-Down
1	"	5	"
1	"	3	"
1	2.8	"	"
1	"	0	"

40 minutes total

5-10 minutes: Brief General Cool-Down & Stretch

As I write this, I did this workout yesterday. In my training diary I noted: "Went very well — felt fine — hard, but I can do more." I mention this to give you an idea of the proper exertion in a "hard" workout. It should be just that, *hard,* but you should come away from the workout feeling that you are capable of an even harder, or "very hard," effort. Remember, the basic purpose of this

12-week routine is to prepare you — physically and mentally — for PR's in the next training cycle.

This workout was my best recent effort in the endurance phase. There's no doubt in my mind, however, that I can do better the next time around. You should feel the same way after a "hard" workout.

Now let's move on to the other "hard" treadmill workouts in this routine.

Remember, the basic purpose of this 12-week routine is to prepare you — physically and mentally — for PR's in the next training cycle. *Photo by Guy Appelman.*

WEEK SIX: DAY TWO
The Strength-and-Endurance Phase
Treadmill — Hard

Same as the "hard" treadmill workout in Week Seven of the first routine (see page 183).

WEEK SEVEN: DAY TWO
The Strength Phase
Treadmill — Hard

Same as the "hard" treadmill workout in Week 11 of the first routine (see page 194).

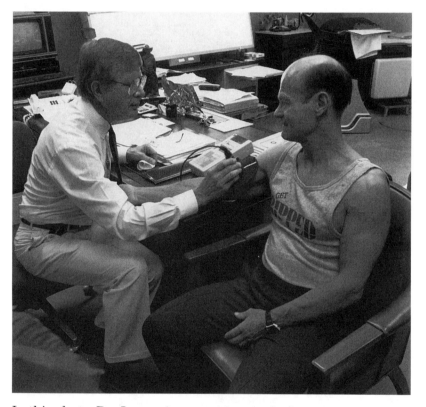

In this photo, Dr. Jensen is measuring my body composition with the Futrex-5000 Body Fat and Fitness Computer. The Cooper Clinic also used fat-fold thickness and underwater weighing to measure my body fat level. I'm scheduled to go back to The Cooper Clinic for further testing later this year. As mentioned earlier, my goal is to perform better on the treadmill at 55 than I did when I was 51. *Photo by Justin Joseph.*

WEEK EIGHT: DAY TWO
The Unload Phase
Treadmill — Easy

This is the same workout as in Week Four, Day Five of this routine. And that brings us to the end of the treadmill sessions. I plan to use these same workouts to prepare for my date with The Cooper Clinic treadmill when I turn 55. I have confidence in these workouts. They work for me. And I'm confident that they will work for you, too.

Now let's go back to Week Five and pick up the Air-Dyne workouts. They begin as the easy-day session in Weeks Five through Seven, and then become the hard day in the final weeks of this training cycle.

WEEK FIVE: DAY FIVE
The Endurance Phase
Air-Dyne — Comfortable

Same as the "comfortable" workout in Week Three of the first routine (see pages 173-174).

WEEK SIX: DAY FIVE
The Strength-and-Endurance Phase
Air-Dyne — Comfortable

Same as the "comfortable" workout in Week Seven of the first routine (see pages 184-185).

WEEK SEVEN: DAY FIVE
The Strength Phase
Air-Dyne — Comfortable

Same as the "comfortable" workout in Week 11 of the first routine (see pages 195-196).

WEEK EIGHT: DAY FIVE
The Unload Phase
Air-Dyne — Easy

Same as the "easy" workout in Week Five of the first routine (see pages 180-181).

That's the end of the easy Air-Dyne sessions; the Air-Dyne becomes the hard-day session in the final weeks of the training cycle. *Photo by Chris Lund.*

WEEK NINE: DAY TWO
The Endurance Phase
Air-Dyne — Hard

Same as the "hard" workout in Weeks Two and Seven of the second routine (see page 212).

WEEK TEN: DAY TWO
The Strength and Endurance Phase
Air-Dyne — Hard

Same as the "hard" workout in Weeks Four and Nine of the second routine (see pages 212-213).

WEEK ELEVEN: DAY TWO
The Strength Phase
Air-Dyne — Hard

Same as the "hard" workout in Weeks Six and 11 of the second routine (see pages 213-214).

WEEK TWELVE: DAY TWO
The Unload Phase
Air-Dyne — Easy

Same as the "easy" workout in Week Five of the first routine (see pages 180-181).

Finally, the "comfortable" rowing sessions on Day Five of Weeks Nine, Ten and 11 are the same as the "comfortable" workouts in the second routine (see pages 214, 217, 218). The "easy" rowing session in Week 12, the unload phase, is the same as the "easy" workout in the second routine (Week 3) on page 217.

*****

Thus we have come to the end of the third and last routine.

At this point, I realize your head may be spinning. Relax! To help you put everything into perspective, we'll conclude with a discussion of what is called "the ownership principle."

That's the end of the routines. Now, let's take a few minutes to put everything into perspective. *Photo by Chris Lund.*

CHAPTER VIII
THE OWNERSHIP PRINCIPLE

Photo by Guy Appelman.

CHAPTER VIII:
THE OWNERSHIP PRINCIPLE

THE OWNERSHIP PRINCIPLE

The shelves at my office and home are lined with books on nutrition and exercise. If you grab any of the books and flip through the pages, you'll find sentences underlined and scribbling in the margins. I don't read a book, I devour it!

Out of all those books, however, I've yet to find one whose content or message I was willing to swallow hook, line and sinker. Instead, from each book, I take what rings true, makes sense, and what I can use — and I leave the rest. So I really don't expect that many people will adopt every aspect of the program presented in this book. And in some ways, as I'll explain in a moment, it's probably best that you don't swallow my message whole.

Several years ago, I struck up a conversation in a bookstore with a fellow browser. If memory serves me correctly, he was a dentist. He recognized me as an author and columnist, and we got to talking about books in general. Something he said has stuck in my mind ever since: "If I get just one idea from a book that I can use," he told me, "I consider it a worthwhile read." Think about it. There's a lot of validity in what he said, isn't there?

It can be said that all of us are the sum total of everything we've read and experienced over the course of our lifetime, not just one book or one experience. The lifestyle we lead is pieced together from many different sources. This point was brought home to me by a series of letters from a 50-year-old Swedish health-and-fitness enthusiast.

At first, I passed this gentleman off as an eccentric. After reading my first book, *Ripped,* when it was serialized in *Bodybuilding Monthly,* a British publication, he expressed a rather off-the-wall (I thought) opinion, "I do not believe that the human body is built to lift weights for sets and repetitions as is done when bodybuilding," he wrote in his first letter. Obviously, I didn't agree. So you can see why I was not instantly attracted to the man and his views. On further reflection and after receiving several more letters, however, it dawned on me that there is an important lesson in what he had to say. Let me tell you a little bit more about him, and why his views are important.

He's no kook. He's had the same job for the last 25 years, working from midnight to around seven in the morning. Plus, he's been an observer of the health-and-fitness scene for almost as long. About 20 years ago, he bought a bodybuilding course and started training. Enclosed with one of his letters was a picture of himself holding a current issue of *Muscle & Fitness,* the world's most widely read bodybuilding magazine, which shows that, in spite of his apparent aversion to weight training, he's still interested in the topic. As mentioned, he took the trouble to read my book when it was spread over several issues of *Bodybuilding Monthly.* So his opinions had been formed over time, and only after long study.

After a year of lifting, he claims, his blood pressure went up. What's more, he sent me a picture of his scar to prove that he got a hernia from deadlifting. That seems to be what persuaded him that the human body — or at least his body — is not built to lift weights. He stopped lifting, but he didn't lose interest in health and fitness, not by a long shot. The muscles he built with weights are all gone now, he says, but his photo shows a very lean and fit 50-year-old. That's no accident.

He has continued to exercise, following a program of simple calisthenics — push-ups, sit-ups, one-legged squats, lunges, neck bridges and the like — developed by Swedish fitness advisor Arne Tammer. In addition, rain or shine, he runs/jogs around a school yard for 15 minutes (no more, no less) two times per week. He runs in the clothes he has on, "even if it's boots and a raincoat." Like I said, he's no casual fitness buff.

His father died of a heart attack at age 53, and it's pretty clear he wants to avoid a similar fate. That's why he never eats meat or any fatty food and doesn't drink milk. Seven days a week, he eats only fish, potatoes, rice, tomatoes, bananas, carrots, bread and drinks nothing but water. That may sound boring, but I believe him when he says he enjoys every meal. As you already know, my own meals follow a regular pattern, too.

Obviously, through trial and error, my Swedish friend has found a diet and exercise program that works for him. He's taken bits and pieces from weight trainers (calisthenics, after all, are a form of weight training), from me (uniform eating), from Arne Tammer and probably a lot of other people. He took what made sense to him and combined it to form his own unique system. It's his personal program and that, no doubt, is why it works so well... for him. He's undergone a psychological process of "ownership." It's a process that often spells the difference between success and failure for those trying to become lean and fit, and stay that way.

As noted in Chapter One, the dismal statistics say that 95% of those who manage to lose weight gain it all back... and then some! Actually, that number exaggerates the failure rate to some extent. "The statistics we have come from clinical settings where you get the people with the toughest problems," says Kelly Brownell, Ph.D., co-director of the Obesity Research Clinic at the University of Pennsylvania. Nevertheless, it's common knowledge that most people are unable to keep the weight from coming back on once they've lost it. Some do succeed, however. When they do, it's generally because they've adopted the ownership principle.

Susan Olson, Director of Psychological Services at the Southwest Geriatric Nutrition Center in Scottsdale, Arizona, and Dr. Robert Colvin of the Southern Illinois University School of Medicine studied 54 adults who had lost at least 20% of their body weight and had maintained that weight loss for a minimum of two years. They found plenty of variation in why and how these people succeeded. But there was one common denominator: these people each found their own method for shedding pounds and keeping them off, a method with which they were comfortable. Like the Swedish gentleman, they didn't rely on someone else's program. They developed their own.

Weigh what I have to say. If common sense tells you it's good advice, and you feel comfortable with the "fit," adapt it to your special situation.

That may sound too simple, but Dr. Olson says that many dieters find it much more comfortable to rely on "external" controls such as weight-loss programs that dictate how to act. That mind set, she says, allows the potential weight loser to feel that it's not really "up to him," that "cheating" reflects upon someone other than himself, that the control, the rules, the entire process are all out of his hands. Besides being untrue, such thoughts undermine a person's confidence in the weight-loss solution. Like the old adage says, "A person convinced against his will is of the same opinion still." That means, of course, that the person soon goes back to his or her old fattening ways.

"It's a matter of what people are really willing and not willing to do," Dr. Olson explained. My Swedish correspondent is not willing to lift weights, but calisthenics, running on the track in all manner of attire — even when it's snowing — and a fat-free diet suit him just fine. That's why the routine works for him. He made the rules, and he alone is responsible for the results. It's his program. He owns it.

That's the reason why I wrote this book with thinking men and women in mind. As explained in Chapter Three, I want readers to focus less on the *how* of my diet and training and more on the *why*.

We all have different backgrounds, needs, goals and abilities. Obviously, no one program is suitable for everyone.

The lifestyle described in this book is mine. I don't expect you to follow it blindly. Weigh what I have to say. If common sense tells you it's good advice, and you feel comfortable with the "fit," adapt it to *your* special situation. Don't rely on someone else's program, including mine. Take that which suits you and leave the rest. Develop your own health and fitness lifestyle. Own it.

Do that, and chances are you'll be Lean For Life.

Don't rely on someone else's program, including mine. Take that which suits you and leave the rest. *Photo by Chris Lund.*

Develop your own health and fitness lifestyle. Own it. Do that, and chances are you'll be Lean For Life. *Photo by Allen Hughes.*

Photo by Allen Hughes.

OTHER BOOKS
BY CLARENCE BASS

THE RIPPED SERIES

Clarence Bass' quest for life-long leanness begins with the *Ripped* series. Your journey should begin there as well.

In *Ripped*, Clarence explains, step-by-step, how he reduced his body fat to 2.4% and won his class in the Past-40 Mr. America contest. This is the basic diet book for bodybuilders and fitness-minded individuals.

Ripped 2 explains staying lean, aerobics, building muscle, peaking, and bodybuilding psychology. Many say it's the best book ever written on weight training.

Ripped 3 contains detailed comments on 22 meal plans that will make and keep you lean. Plus, it's the break-through book on periodization training for bodybuilders.

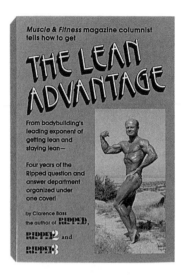

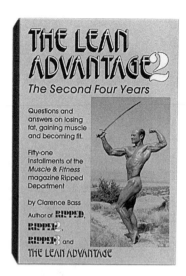

THE LEAN ADVANTAGE SERIES

Do you have question about losing fat, getting fit, healthy lifestyle, aging, or anything related to diet and exercise?

Chances are the answers are in *The Lean Advantage* series, where 155 installments of Clarence Bass' popular question and answer column, The Ripped Department, are collected. Taken together, the three books (The Lean Advantage 1, 2 & 3) constitute a virtual encyclopedia of the bodybuilding and fitness lifestyle.

Here are some of the topics covered: body fat tests, successful dieting, muscle building, aerobics, exercise physiology, motivation, preventable diseases, aging, and much, much more.

The lifestyle approach to leanness
- Balanced Diet
- Aerobic Exercise
- Weight Training

By CLARENCE BASS

LEAN FOR LIFE

The fitness trend of the new century is balanced training—strength and endurance. Clarence Bass leads the way with *LEAN FOR LIFE*. He explains, day-by-day, how to combine weights and aerobics to achieve total fitness. What's more, he shows how to stay motivated—and lean—forever. He presents a lifestyle approach that will make you lean for life.

Don't miss a single step on the road to permanent leanness. Read all of Clarence Bass' books.

Turn page for more information and where to order.

Clarence Bass'

RIPPED™ Enterprises

We are your source for bodybuilding, fitness, health, motivation, diet and fat loss information.

Please visit us on the Internet at
http://www.cbass.com

You'll find not only information about our books and other products, but also more about Clarence Bass' background and training career, his diet and training philosophy in brief, frequently asked questions, late news — and new articles by Clarence Bass (a new article at the beginning of each month).

Ripped Enterprises
P.O. Box 51236
Albuquerque, NM 87181-1236 USA
Phone: 505-266-5858
Fax: 505-266-9123

Also available from
Clarence Bass' RIPPED Enterprises

❖ Posing Trunks

❖ Women's
   Posing Suits

❖ Audio tapes

❖ Videos and DVDs

❖ Color Photos

❖ Food
   Supplements

❖ Selected
   Books

❖ Personal
   Consultations

Model: Dorine Tilton

Clarence Bass' RIPPED Enterprises
P.O. Box 51236
Albuquerque, NM 87181-1236 USA
Phone: 505-266-5858 / Fax: 505-266-9123

E-mail: cncbass@aol.com
Web site: http://www.cbass.com

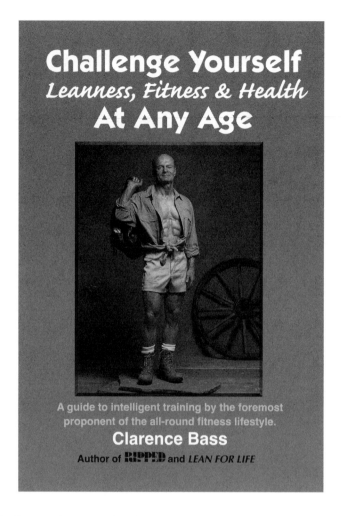

Challenge Yourself
Leanness, Fitness & Health
At Any Age

A guide to intelligent training by the foremost
proponent of the all-round fitness lifestyle.
Clarence Bass
Author of **RIPPED** and *LEAN FOR LIFE*

Challenge Yourself is Clarence Bass' latest book. The key to becoming—and staying— lean, fit, and healthy is to continually challenge yourself in an intelligent and thoughtful way. That's what this book is about. It explains how Clarence has continued to improve for more than 45 years—and how you can follow suit. The other books get you started and this book will keep you going.

Cutting edge, ***Challenge Yourself*** includes psychologically sound techniques for staying motivated, the latest developments in diet and nutrition, detailed new routines for beginners and intermediates (weights only), Clarence's current routine, athlete-type strength training, high-intensity aerobics, longevity and health topics, and exciting personal profiles.